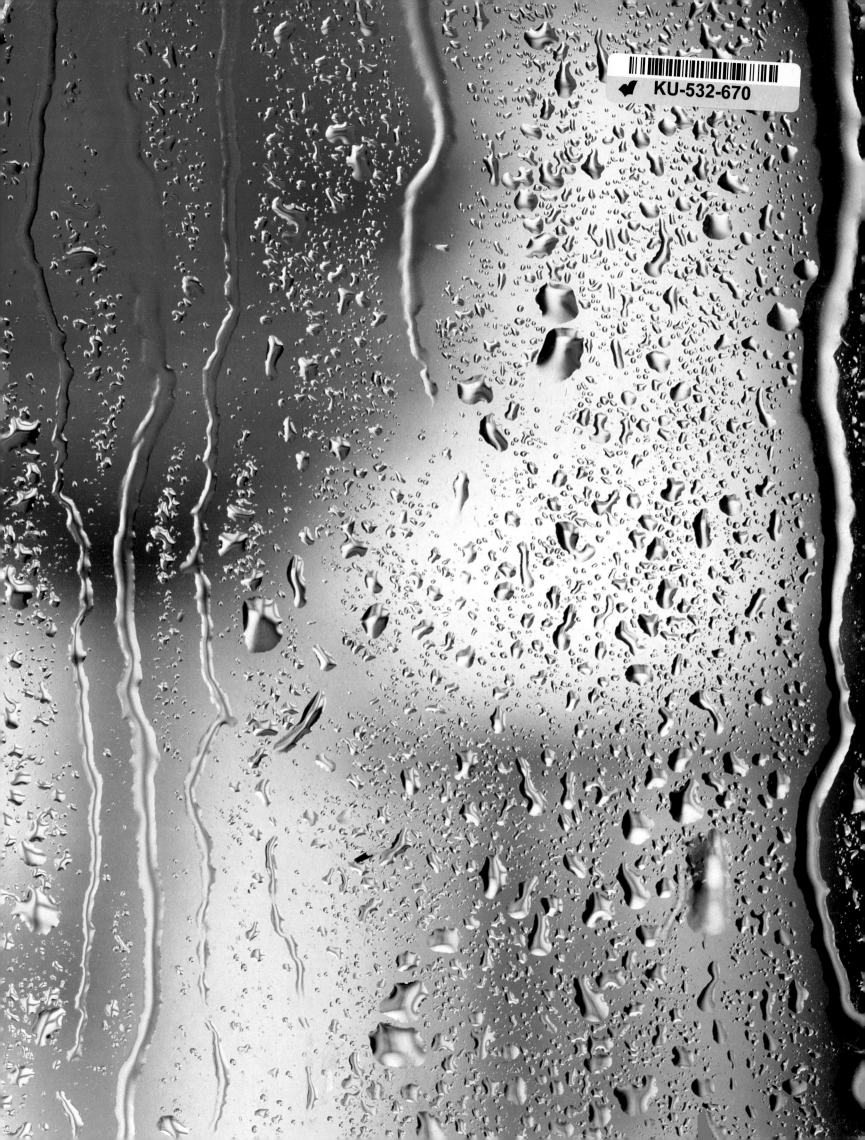

B

BLAG™

Blag
MADE IN ENGLAND

BLAG
WORLDWIDE
INDUSTRIES
INCORPORATED
PLC

2000

P.96 Pharcyde

P.5 Airports

P.14 Redman

P.88 Kung Fu

P.20 Giant

P.78 New York

P.24 Black Eyed Peas

P.74 Prince Paul

P.30 UK

P.66 The Roots

P.36 UK Motorways

P.58 Auto

P.40 St.Petersburg B-Boys

P.50 Coasters

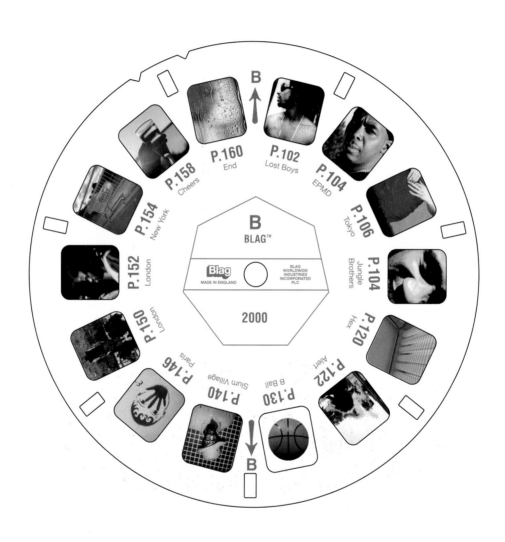

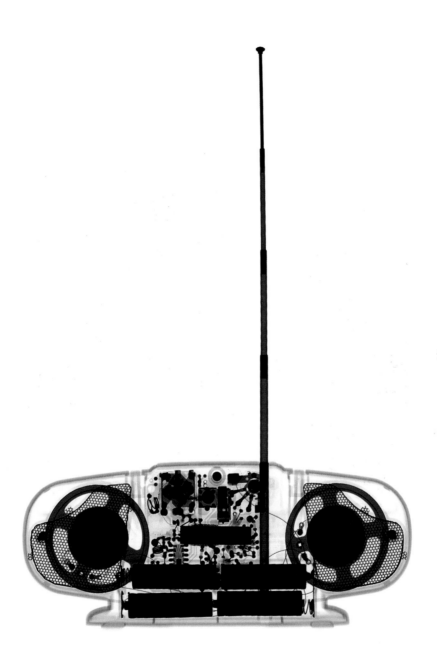

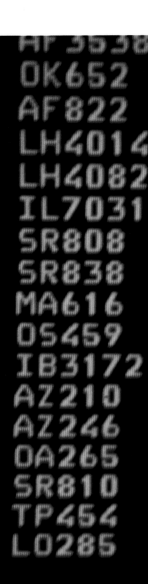

40	Prague	OK652	Landed	22
10	Paris-CdG	AF822	Landed	22
15	Frankfurt	LH4014	Landed	22
30	Munich	LH4082	Landed	22
35	Istanbul	IL7031	Landed	22
40	Zurich	SR808	Landed	22
45	Geneva	SR838	Landed	22
05	Budapest	MA616	Landed	22
05	Vienna	OS459	Landed	22
10	Madrid	IB3172	Landed	22
20	Rome	AZ210	Landed	21
25	Milan	AZ246	Expected	21
30	Athens	OA265	Expected	21
40	Zurich	SR810	Landed	21
45	Lisbon	TP454	Expected	21
60	Warsaw	LO285	Expected	22

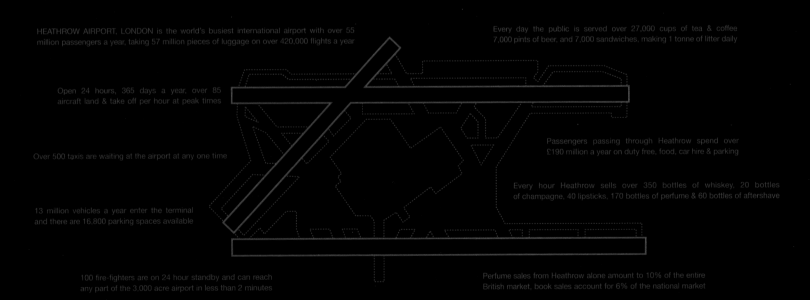

HEATHROW AIRPORT, LONDON is the world's busiest international airport with over 55 million passengers a year, taking 57 million pieces of luggage on over 420,000 flights a year

Every day the public is served over 27,000 cups of tea & coffee 7,000 pints of beer, and 7,000 sandwiches, making 1 tonne of litter daily

Open 24 hours, 365 days a year, over 85 aircraft land & take off per hour at peak times

Over 500 taxis are waiting at the airport at any one time

Passengers passing through Heathrow spend over £190 million a year on duty free, food, car hire & parking

Every hour Heathrow sells over 350 bottles of whiskey, 20 bottles of champagne, 40 lipsticks, 170 bottles of perfume & 60 bottles of aftershave

13 million vehicles a year enter the terminal and there are 16,800 parking spaces available

100 fire-fighters are on 24 hour standby and can reach any part of the 3,000 acre airport in less than 2 minutes

Perfume sales from Heathrow alone amount to 10% of the entire British market, book sales account for 6% of the national market

Grass on the airport is kept constantly at 8 inches high to avoid birds settling, at this height the birds can not spot predators so do not land

The Swatch Shop sells 78,000 watches a year from a space the size of an average sitting room

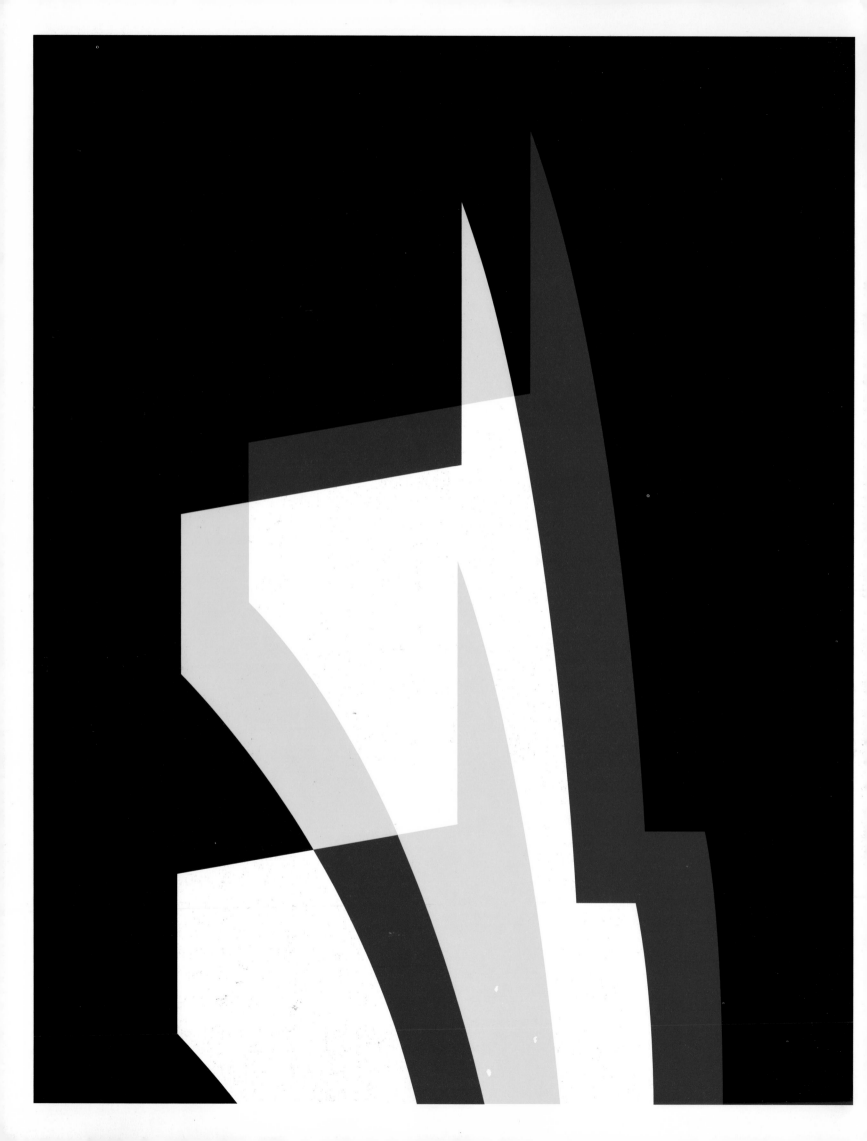

REDMAN

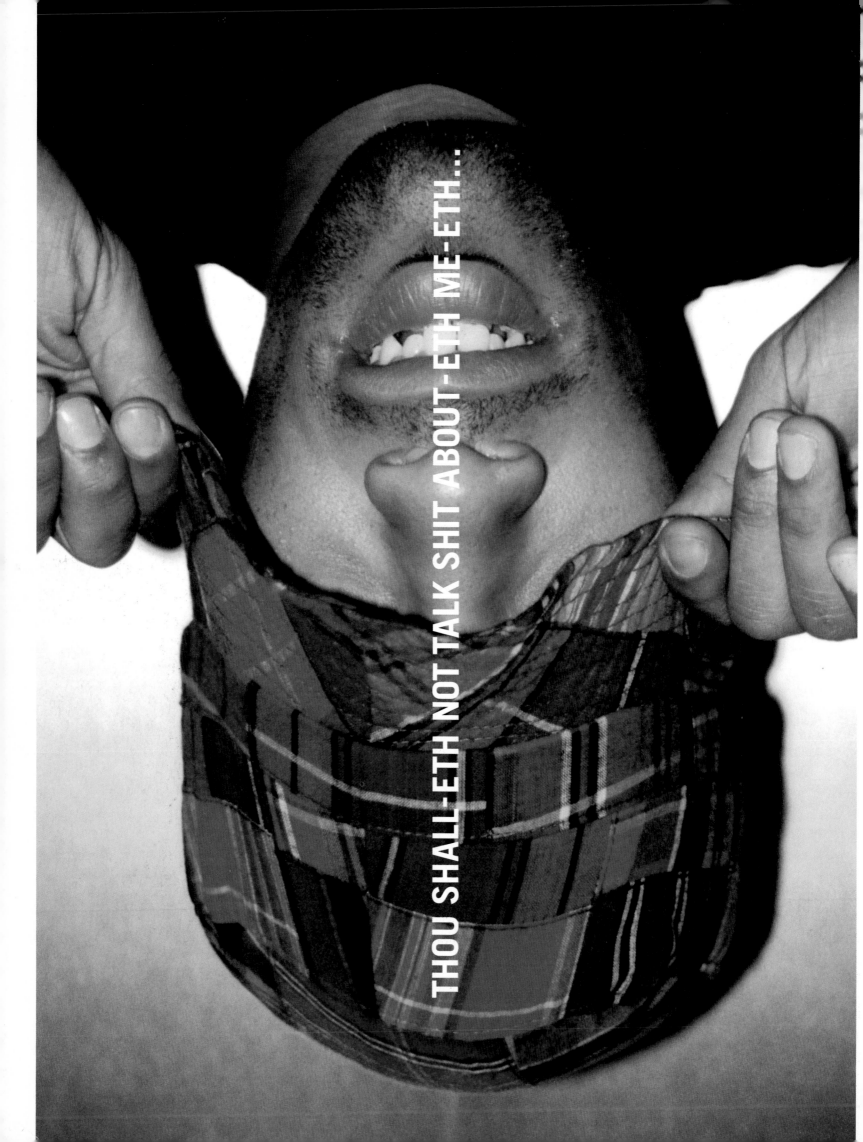

THOU SHALL-ETH NOT TALK SHIT ABOUT-ETH ME-ETH...

OK Inhale.....exhale.....hi(gh)... So, tell me who's Reggie Noble? "Well, Reggie Noble is more the business end." He's charismatic, melismatic... the producer, the transducer... *"I'll bee dat."* So, who's Funk Doc? He's sharp witted, high spirited, the funk possesor... *"... the roughest rapper a turntable needle ever came across." "I'll bee dat"* And Redman? "He's the more active person, he handles the stage and the mics" Loves the blunt... exeunt. *"I'll bee dat."* Bring the ruckus & the charas to all you motherf***ers... Welcome to the world of Redman.

Can you tell me a bit about where you grew up and your funniest childhood memory? "Where I grew up? I grew up in Newark, New Jersey... and the most what?" And your funniest childhood memory? ..sighs... "Damn. I didn't have too many fun childhood memories. What do you mean? What I did that was the funnest?" Well, yeah it can be. "Um, I don't know I guess the first time I smoked weed. Yeah, the first time I smoked weed."

Alright, can you tell us what your own version of the ten commandments would be? "My own version of the ten commandments?" Yeah. "I'd have thou shall not kill. Thou shall-eth smoketh weedeth... ha ha ha... thou shall-eth not mindeth my business. Thou shall-eth not get jealous. Thou shall-eth always love music. Thou shall-eth...ah, let me see, thou shall love ya mama. Thou shall prosper tha life. Thou shall-eth not talk shit about me-th, cos if you do-eth, I'm a kick-eth your ass-eth... Heh heh heh. And how many was that?" Eight. "Let me see... Thou shall-eth keep-eth a healthy mind. Thou shall-eth always love women."

Can you let us in on the continuation of the 'Whateva Man' video? "The continuation of 'Whateva Man' video? I don't know, it might be a Method Man track or something. We might continue the video from his album, when he comes out with it, you know? So I don't know how that's gonna go, but it's gonna continue on his shit though. Unless, it's gonna continue on my next album...yeah."

Tell us about your collaborations together with K-Solo and Method Man? "Well, working with them is not hard. Working with Method Man is just like working with me all over, you know what I'm sayin' just working with another... 'cos we rhyme the same way. You know, we look at things in life the same way, we're on the same label. Whereas though K-Solo is the same thing, you know, he's more older though, so working with him... first of all working with him, we didn't intend to make that record ("It's Like That (My Big Brother)") like that, it just happened. When I worked with Meth we knew what we was gonna do, you know we sat down and wrote it and we knew that shit was gonna be hot, because we got two different styles, but we're on the same level. With the Solo, we just rhymed you know what I'm sayin', we just did some back in the day freestyles... just makin' it happen, and we made it happen and it came out hot and you know we didn't know it was gonna be hot, it just came out hot."

Can you make up a cocktail and tell us the ingredients and name? "A cocktail? Yeah! Oh I don't know... Shit! I don't really drink... I can't drink, but if I had to make a cocktail I'd make a little Hennessy, a little Alize and a little er... Oh! Hennessy, Alize and Ginger Ale." Cool, what would you call it? "I'd call it Gennezzy... heh heh heh ha ha ha!"

OK, say you had to do an advert for TV, for headache pills. Can you make up what the headache pills are called and do the advert? "I'd be like, I'd have the pills like this *(pretends to hold the pills up near his face)*, and I'd just be like you know... I'd be like 'If you had a bad day, you had a baaad night, shit just wasn't goin' right, Motherf***ers f*** with you outta spite, try these new pills called D.F. 'ill "Don't F*** Wit Me, Pills". If you're tired of Motherf***ers coming into you (probably in the morning, with their stink breath) knowing you don't feel like being bothered, you just wanna sit down and have a nutritious day to get rid of your headache, try D.F. 'ill. And it also comes with a T-Shirt "Don't F*** With Me" and it'll work. And the T-Shirt'll say "Don't F*** Wit Me or you must have taken you Don't F*** With Me pills" Yeah. So, you know what to do, don't even come around 'cos my attitude is real nauseous. Word.'"

OK, can you give us a rough guide to New York including places to eat, drink, shop and go out. "In New York?" Yeah. "Yeah, you can eat at City Crab, or you can go right Uptown to The Jamaica Hot Pot. They sell curry, shrimp and rice and maize. If you wanna have a good time - Shit! - go right to the hood. You'll see a lot of shit happening. Motherf***ers running, Motherf***ers' cars crashing. Go get some good weed Uptown. Come back

Downtown and go to the Tunnel on Sunday, where all the freaks is at. And a have a luscious weekend. For real."

Alright, you know there's loads of laws, like drinking laws, are there any if those you'd want to change, if you get the opportunity? "Yeah, I'd change the driving laws. I'd change the driving laws around, I'd change the... let me see, what else? I wouldn't change the smoking laws. I wouldn't legalise it; I like sneaking around smoking. If everybody could smoke, then what the f***?! Everybody would be high everyday. I'd change the probation laws too. Instead of taking the pee test to see if you don't smoke, I'd have a pee test to see if you do smoke! And the suspended license, I'd just be like 'license not suspended.' You'd just get pulled over, 'Oh you hit that person's back tyre? Go ahead give them some money and be on you way.' I'd just change a whole lot of shit around, 'cos motherf***ers are getting locked up too. I'd change the gun law, what else? That's about it right now."

Okay, have you got any predictions for Hip Hop music and style? And which way will it all be heading? "To me, I don't know. Lately I haven't been feeling Hip Hop. I guess it's just going through that phase. There ain't too much shit that's exciting me that much, I don't know. I mean it's gonna grow, it'll grow more and more. Through the media there's going to be a lot more bullshit happening to rappers too. Plus it's going to be more political, so you've just gotta come out with a commercial record to even sell shit, 'cos that hardcore shit is just keepin' niggas at one level, so now niggas think they've got to always make something pop or commercial to get on the air. And it's gonna get worse. There's gonna be more violence, but it's gonna be around the whole world, you're gonna see a lot of Motherf***ers doing it and making money off of it too. We're gonna see a lot more young CEO's too."

Can you tell us three expressions that really irritate you? "What like if somebody tells you something that you usually hear?" Yeah. "Oh, okay... like if when you walk into a hotel and the f***in' security ask you, 'Are you registered here?' I hate that shit. 'No, motherf***er, I'm just here to do your job. Heh heh heh. 'Um, let me see. I hate it when the cops say 'License and Registration please.' I hate that expression, I really do. And I hate when somebody asks me 'Am I Redman?' I hate it, hate it

to a T. I hate it to a T. 'Are you Redman?' No! No, that ain't me! Heh heh heh!"

Can you tell us three words that you'd use to sum yourself up? "Funky, Self-Confident and Confident."

While touring, what will you be listening to and watching on the tour bus? "I'll be watching Predator, listening to old CD's, like the... old tapes, old CD's of old artists; some Hip Hop. And I'll be watching Predator, Dead Presidents, National Lampoons Vacation...Ha ha ha!... Ace Ventura Pet Detective 1 & 2... Let me see, a couple of pornos. Yeah, that's about it - shit! *(out of the blue, Redman slips into a London accent)* 'Yeah that's about it' - or some of my shows I have recorded on tour."

That's all my questions is there anything else you want to add? "Yeah, I wanna add that I will come over and rock the house. I'm glad that London supported me for all four albums, 'cos a lot of Motherf***ers is really big fans over there. I'd like to say to everyone who supported me over there, one love and I'll see ya'll wit da stankin' asses!"

Contains lyrical excerpts from 'Doc's Da Name 2000' by Redman.

Giant & Ser Trackside near Anerley South London

22nd & Illinois San Francisco

4 Hills Albuquerque

Oakland California

Muni Graveyard

Outside Tokyo

Oakland

N Judah Tunnel San Francisco

Giant & Vez South Chicago

3rd & 4th San Francisco

TOP TEN PLACES TO PAINT

Metal Wall @ 22nd & Illinois, San Francisco
South London Tracksides
Tokyo
Trainyard in Oakland, California
Four Hills Ditch, Albuquerque New Mexico
N Judah Tunnel, San Francisco
The Oakland Tracks
Muni Graveyard, San Francisco
South Chicago
Wall @ 3rd & 4th, San Francisco

BLACK EY

ED PEAS

Black Eyed Peas from LA, California are in London. They did a show a couple of nights ago and have been amusing themselves for the last couple of days. We at blag arranged with Will to put a stop to that and let you know what they're all about. Sarah and I catch up with him on a cold rainy night at their hotel. The story begins at reception: **"Hello I'm here to do an interview with one of your guests, I was asked to call first but the phone's been engaged for a while now. Can you check if it's okay please?"**, I ask. "Oh, I have a message here that you should just go to his room", replies the lady behind the desk. "I'd rather you asked first, I don't want to intrude." *So she tries for me and the line is still engaged; she then sends us to his room. Sarah and I make sceptical tracks in fear of invading a private phone call. We get to the door look at each other with 'Here goes' written all over our faces and I proceed to knock (that regular rhythm you'll all be familiar with). The door is opened by Will who seems taller than at the show the other night* "Hello!" *I smile.* "Hey, come in…" *he replies, then goes back over to his laptop which is set up in the corner.* "I'll be with you in a moment." *He's on the Internet, writing e-mails (that'll be why the phone was engaged). After a while of sitting around, the laptop is put to sleep and we have Will's full attention.*

So here we go: **Please introduce yourself, including your name and where you come from.** My name is Will.I.Am, I come from my Mum's womb. Your supposed to say where you live! Oh, I live in Los Angeles, California. East Los Angeles, which is predominately filled with Hispanics and Chicanos.

Describe the other members of Black Eyed Peas. Well, there's Taboo Nawasha and Apl De Ap. Taboo's the Indian, the native American cat. Apl De Ap is the black Filipino.

Tell me the history of Black Eyed Peas. Like real quick or take like an hour? Real Quick. Okay, before we were Black Eyed Peas, Apl and myself were signed to Ruthless Records as a group called Atban Klann, and we never came out because we were on a predominately gangsta label. We were the only group besides Blood Abraham that wasn't gangsta, and they didn't know how to promote and market us - which is a blessing - so we never came out. Then we started Black Eyed Peas in 1995. The first label didn't want to sign us. They said "Well, The Roots, they don't really sell records, and the only reason De La and Tribe sell records is because they're De La and Tribe, so what makes you think you guys are gonna sell records? And The Pharcyde doesn't sell records either, and they're from LA, so what makes you think you're gonna sell records in your hometown?" They didn't really believe in it, so in 1996 we shopped again, and they still didn't really want to sign us. Then in the beginning of 1997 we shopped, and we had like 'Joints And Jam', 'Fallin' Up', 'Head Bobs', 'The Way U Make Me Feel' and 'Positivity' - we shopped those songs and they still didn't want to sign us, so then we was like "F*** it, why don't you want to sign us? There must be something wrong?" So we went out to colleges, like round LA, UCLA, USC, Northbridge, Long Beach… all the colleges… and at Loyal and Maramount we met our keyboard and guitarist, and recorded even more songs there because the keyboardist was a teacher there, and he used to let us use the studio for free, and we used to sneak in and record more songs. Then we met the guy that directs all our videos, Brian Beletic there at that college. And I was like "Let's just keep doing these shows at colleges, because all the people at these colleges are eventually going to be the people running the world." Do you know what I mean? Colleges are like preschool to the world, so because of that there's people who are at college who intern at record companies and word got around "Oh I'm gonna see Black Eyed Peas at Dragonfly." We were playing club dates in Hollywood, LA, where we created a buzz and a following of college kids and Interscope came knocking on our door again and they caught the vapours…like Biz Markie!

What makes Black Eyed Peas different from other Hip Hop groups including Philosophies and Lyrics. Well, our personalities, and because we let our personalities shine through our music, and that's the first thing we do; there really is no gimmick or image. We're not like (Will screws up his face and does impressions of various heads) 'Oh we the hardcore kids outta LA, 'cos everything outta LA is gangsta, so we the hardcore motherf****ers you know, you know keeping it real with whats the streets' talkin' about.' Like you know 'We for the ladies you know, 'cos the ladies want to hear some love hip hop too so…' or 'We're the first hip hop band outta LA!' You know we don't really want to put cliches there, you know? We're just us, and because we put our personalities first and we try to make our audience get to know us that's what makes us different; because you know I'm not Black Thought and Taboo's not Q-Tip, he's Taboo, and through our personal taste and influences that makes the Peas. Coool! That was a good answer huh? Ha ha!

Talk about your style, dress sense and stage presence. The way I dress personally, that's what I prefer. Like a lot of cats think "Oh, he's just put the clothes on before the show and before he starts the video." But it's like I wake up and I put on the shirt, or I wake up and these are the only tennis shoes I have and they're not even tennis shoes, I don't even own a pair of white socks. I just bought this horse shirt, it's made out of horse skin - pretty fly! I bought it in Piccadilly. You know it's not even like you can see it! (Will rubs it on the mic of the tape recorder.) Ha ha! So when I go riding my horse you know we can match! Ha ha ha! And Stage Presence? Stage presence is a rebellion against the norm. Normal Hip Hop groups don't really take into consideration the people who bought your album. You got to make them go home and feel like they've invested their money in the right place. You know these are fans that are supporting your career, these are the people that are responsible for that nice watch and that nice car, and you buying your Mum and your girlfriend shit. They are responsible for you coming to other countries, so if you don't take into mind - "Okay, wow! I gotta make these people feel like they've invested their money", or just put on, entertain them even if they haven't bought your CD - they could have gone to see - you know Dru Hill or another group, but they're at your show. Even if they're like "Well f*** 'em, I'm just here to see if dem fools is real." So because of that, make them not go home "Yeah I knew they was wack, soft ass niggas with their thrift store clothes." You know what I mean? Don't make them go home and say that, make them be like "Wow! Yo they dress funny and shit, yo but they can rock a crowd." So I remember going to see my favourite artists and I'm like "Wooh habahabahaba woooooh hehe I'm going to see woooh it's gonna be-dope-be-dope-be-dope!!!" And I'd be disappointed like "Damn! they sucked." I'd rather stay home and listen to the CD and move it like he-he (Will moves his hand from side-to-side). Ha ha ha! You know and then they get mad if you're not clapping and responding. Then a lot of Hip Hop groups is like "F*** y'all anyway, y'all don't know what the f***…" You know what I mean it's wack. How are you gonna react to an audience when they're not moving? It's not their fault - it's yours. You know don't cuss at them, cuss at yourself. So we reflect personality you know?

What do you think of London, do you get to spend much time here? Tell me your best experience so far. London's cool. I just don't really know too many people here, you know what I mean? For me to enjoy a town I have to know its little peoples. So you know, I can walk around and look at the pretty buildings all day and stuff but it's still going to be boring. So half of the time the cities I go to I'm always on the Internet, or I'm chatting, or writing or thinking of what song to record next. But London's nice, I like the vibe and the people are really cool - you know that's the audience when we perform, they receive us pretty well, but I like to know people on a personal level to enjoy the cities; then they can take me to the places they like you know what I mean, but eventually I'm gonna meet some cats.

Tell us the top 5 tunes to drive to… Hip Hop tunes or songs? Any that you like driving to. I like to listen to 'En Melody' by Serge Gainsbourgh. You never heard of Serge Gainsbourgh? Oh wow man! He's a French cat, an old cat, Jewish cat - he's dope. You know 'De La Soul Is Dead' the album? You know 'Talkin' Bout Hey Love'? Well that background beat is Serge Gainsbourgh, he does a lot of stuff like that - he's dope. Jorge Ben, a Brazilian cat. He had a song called 'Mas Que Nada'. What else? A Tribe Called Quest 'Midnight Marauder' the whole album is like a song to me. Bob James' 'Nautilus' and Billy Brooks' '40 Days'. What got me into this past big variety of music is Tribe Called Quest and De La Soul… Because in 1992 I wanted to start producing, and then I started listening to their stuff to see where they got their samples from, and then hearing on 'Midnight Marauders' the 'Interlude' you know "Tribe Called Quest is…" you know, the background music is Cal Tjader and I was like "Man! How come they didn't use this part?" and then I became a big Cal Tjader fan. Then I started listening to Sergio Mendes, and you know from reading the back of the records I became a fan of different kinds of music. You know not only Brazillian and not only Hip Hop, you know Latin Jazz, French music, Folk music… One shit I ain't got into is country and new R'n'B… Mmm that's one thing I can't mess with. Everything is cookie cutter. Everything is *what?!* Cookie Cutter! It's like a familiar shape and a familiar taste. In order for them to market it they're like "Oh you want circles? Here's some more circles." It's like "I want a triangle! Can I get an Octagon?" You know ha hah!

Throw a dice to reveal a subject to talk about. Alright, I bet you it's gonna be a three. Watch… and then we not gonna talk about the number, we're gonna talk about my ESP. *(Will throws it and gets a 6.)*

6: Stories from School. In 6th grade I had this teacher named Mr. Wright. How old are you in 6th grade? We don't have grades. Oh you don't have grades? Damn! if you're 6 in first grade then you're 7… 12. I don't know… 6 and 7 in first grade, 7 and 8 in second. Okay, if I graduated in 12th grade I was 18, 11th grade I was 17, 10th grade I was 16, 9th grade I was 15, 8th grade I was 14… I was 12 in 6th grade! Wow! You have the ESP! So when I was in 6th grade, at 12 years old, I had this teacher named Mr.Wright, and he was a hippy back when he was my age. So Mr.Wright, he always used to tell us…because I went to Brentwood Science Magnet School, it was like a higher placement, because I lived in the projects you know in East LA, like the ghetto, Chicano ghetto, but I was bust out to a magnet programme because I was a little smarter than my neighbourhood cats. So, I went to this magnet school and not only did they teach science, math blah blah blah, but they taught you astrology and oceanography in Elementary school, and drugs and all that stuff. So he used to tell us about how he did Acid and Mushrooms and we're just little 6th kids and he's like "I could teach you how to get high without getting high…" and out of that, out of him being our teacher, that's why I don't smoke. He never really taught us to get high without getting high, but with him putting that thought in me at that early age… I mean it's so possible especially nowadays cats misuse it, I mean it's cool if you smoke, but I can't do it. It's not good for me, it's like putting water in a gas tank - I conk out and I'm not productive. Oh oh oh!! And he was… the Wright brothers, the ones who invented the airplane? He's their Great Great Great Great Nephew! Hot shit! Yeah yeah yeah!!!

Okay. Do it again and don't get a 6, get a 3. Hehe! *(A 3 is rolled and Will high fives.)* Three's my favourite number! **3: Best and worst places from travels.** So why you have me rolling that dice? I didn't know you were definitely going to get a 3! Oh! Oh I thought… ha ha! Okay, best and worst places is one place, for the best and the worst it's Hamburg, Germany. It's the best place because we got really accepted well there, and we played for like three and a half hours - and you know I've never seen no Hip Hop show for no three and a half hours - and they didn't let us go, they kept on asking for encores, we went on at like 10:30 and didn't get out off 'til like 3, and if that equals three and a half hours then… Good maths! Yeah ha ha ha! So, the vibe was sooo… I was performing, but I was watching us perform. We were freestyling we made up half our new album up there, we made like four songs up. It was packed when we got there and the same amount of people were there when we left, and everybody was like "Yo, I never seen anything like that, I never felt anything like that." It was the bomb! And it's also the worst because they got a little red light district there. I didn't go but my colleague went and he's black - and he was walking through one of those alleyways and then they knock on the window, and then 'Motives' our DJ walks by and the girl was like "Urrgh! Get away." And then we went to McDonalds and there was a white cat in front of us and one at the back of us actually, and we were next to get our Chicken or whatever we was going to order and he told us to move and helped the other cat, and then

WE LET OUR PERSONALITIES SHINE THROUGH OUR MUSIC AND THAT'S THE FIRST THING WE DO, THERE REALLY IS NO GIMMICK OR IMAGE. WILL.I.AM

Moreal got all heated and he's like "F*** this man d'you see what he did?" and I'm like "Man don't worry about it, why are you going to even let them know that it's affected you? You just made balance what just happened, you shouldn't worry about it, you know there's more intelligent people you can get food from." Him doing that is God working in ways you know, him not eating that, he could've choked or got some chicken disease or some shit. You know what I mean? It's sad that there's ignorance out there in this day, but just as much as there's ignorance there's also intelligence - and we just so happened to be in the ignorant part. So, that was the worst experience I've ever had.

1: Previous jobs I've never had a job before in my life. Really?! Oh yes I have, but it wasn't really a job. Back in 1991, me and Apl wanted to buy scooters like Vespas so we got a telecom service job, you know answering telephones: "Hello, this is police activities league may I help you?" And we never made those calls, we used to call our friends "Okay, wassup?......Oh I'm chillin'" so we never got enough money to buy our scooters. We only worked for two weeks; we got fired. Oh, and when I was a kid I used to work with little kids on summer youth programmes, you know go on picnics and shit. You know it's cool, but at the same time it's not you know? At some time I'll be asked out if the music industry changes or we fall off, but that's why I educated myself and went to college and took piano courses because if you want to be a producer you can't just sample all the time. I mean that's not even called a producer that's called a technical guy that just so happens to have taste in music, it's like 'I want to be a song writer/producer' blah blah blah. I don't just want to be sampling so I went to school took a piano course to learn and educate myself, just in case something happens I still have my music to fall back on… Want me to roll another one? If you like… Rolls: No. Rolls: No. Rolls: No.

5: What's the best footwear to dance in for ladies and men. Footwear? Well I don't know too much about girls' shoes, I don't know what it's like to wear some high heels and if I did this interview should be different from now on! Ha ha! You know I don't really know much about girls' shoes but I know they got a better selection as for taste; I mean guys have square shit to choose from. Shoes. I could dance in any shoes, sometimes the slippier the better. I don't like tennis shoes I don't like wearing those, but anything that's slippy enough so it looks like I'm floating… It's cool. So have you had any accidents in slippy shoes? Yeah, I chipped my tooth! No I didn't chip it I was joking! Is it not chipped? Yeah, it's chipped. How did you chip it then? Oh, riding a skate board. I fell off my bike when I was 7. Yeah!? I was 10 when I chipped mine. When you breathed out of your mouth did it hurt? Yeah, and I cut my lip and my neighbour picked me up and said that my tooth would grow back! So, my tooth's split, it's coated in clear stuff. My lips didn't even get hurt, I had to go down smiling, it amazed me that I didn't bust my lips or anything. So yeah. Ha hah!

2: Tell us a dance routine for people to get by on, who aren't that confident or want to impress someone. Oh, I'm anti-routine, anybody can learn a routine. Not like a boy band in the middle of a club or anything, just something to give them a bit more confidence so they're not wall flowers when they go out. Not that we're asking and can't dance! Um… I don't know. Most of the time when me, and Ap and Taboo go out and dance at clubs people don't dance, they watch, you know 'cos we're cutting up a rug, so we're like and they're like "Wow!" So wrong person to ask.

4: Five tips for a good night out. Out on the Internet? Ha ha ha! Five tips… Bring some good friends, so if you're at the wackest club or the wackest bar you just have a whole bunch of laughs; you know you could be at the bus stop and it would be the best. So, take your best friends. That's the best tip… I can't think of anything else. Oh, if you're gonna drink and you're driving make sure one of your friends isn't drinking. If you're a girl and you go out, be respectable. Half the times when cats go up to you in a club it's because they want one thing and one thing only, and if you're cool with that then that's cool, but if you're expecting anything else then don't be played, and if you're drunk make sure your friend isn't and ask her to watch your back, you know I've seen drunk chicks and their friends is kinda skanky anyway and they let themselves get taken advantage of. So you know, make sure you go with somebody that's a good friend, and if the DJs playing wack music: Five wack songs then it's time to go.

2: Tricks on Tour - what do you get up to on tour to while away the time, or do you just go on the internet all the time?! Yeah, or I play Tomb Raider! You know that girl? She's pretty dope… Or I write… Or we… Don't you play any tricks on each other? Oh! Like we'll be walking down the street and we'll say like "Oh check that out!" and we'll stick our elbow out and make them run into it - like "Uh!" That's a trick we always play on each other, and I'm the one that always gets got, 'cos I'm not really aware and my chest gets kinda sore. Telephone bills is always high on the road - so that's a good thing to do is talk on the 'phone, waste your PD on 'phone calls. Ha hah!… Damn!

So that's the end of our interview. It's now time to get Apl De Ap and Taboo for the photo shoot. Will calls their room "You ready? For the photo shoot? The lights are all set up!" Will puts the 'phone down laughing, then picks it up and calls through again: "Bring five changes of clothes okay?!" and hangs up laughing even more. We sit and wait. In the meantime a call comes in for Will, who starts to do an English accent, and the only way he does it is to tip his head back, screw his face up and sound like a girl! Now that's pretty funny, he's like "Mmmmhellow… Mmmmmyesss…" etc. Soon we hear the other pair outside, only they don't knock on the door I think they were kicking it because it just booms. Sarah opens the door and says "Can you do a better British accent than him?" They walk in looking pensive. Introductions take place. Apl sits opposite me and looks through blag and Taboo sits in the most coordinated outfit I've seen and looks at another copy. While Will gets changed in his bathroom singing in an English accent, Taboo apologises for Will's behaviour with a straight face, but Sarah and I are finding him pretty damn amusing. Then, he re-enters the room all dressed up in his new jacket. His next impression is of horses as we leave the room to take the shots. "Hey, we should go riding when we get back home." Marvellous.

I JUST BOUGHT THIS HORSE SHIRT, IT'S MADE OUT OF HORSE SKIN - PRETTY FLY I BOUGHT IT IN PICCADILLY…SO WHEN I GO RIDING MY HORSE YOU KNOW WE CAN MATCH! WILL.I.AM

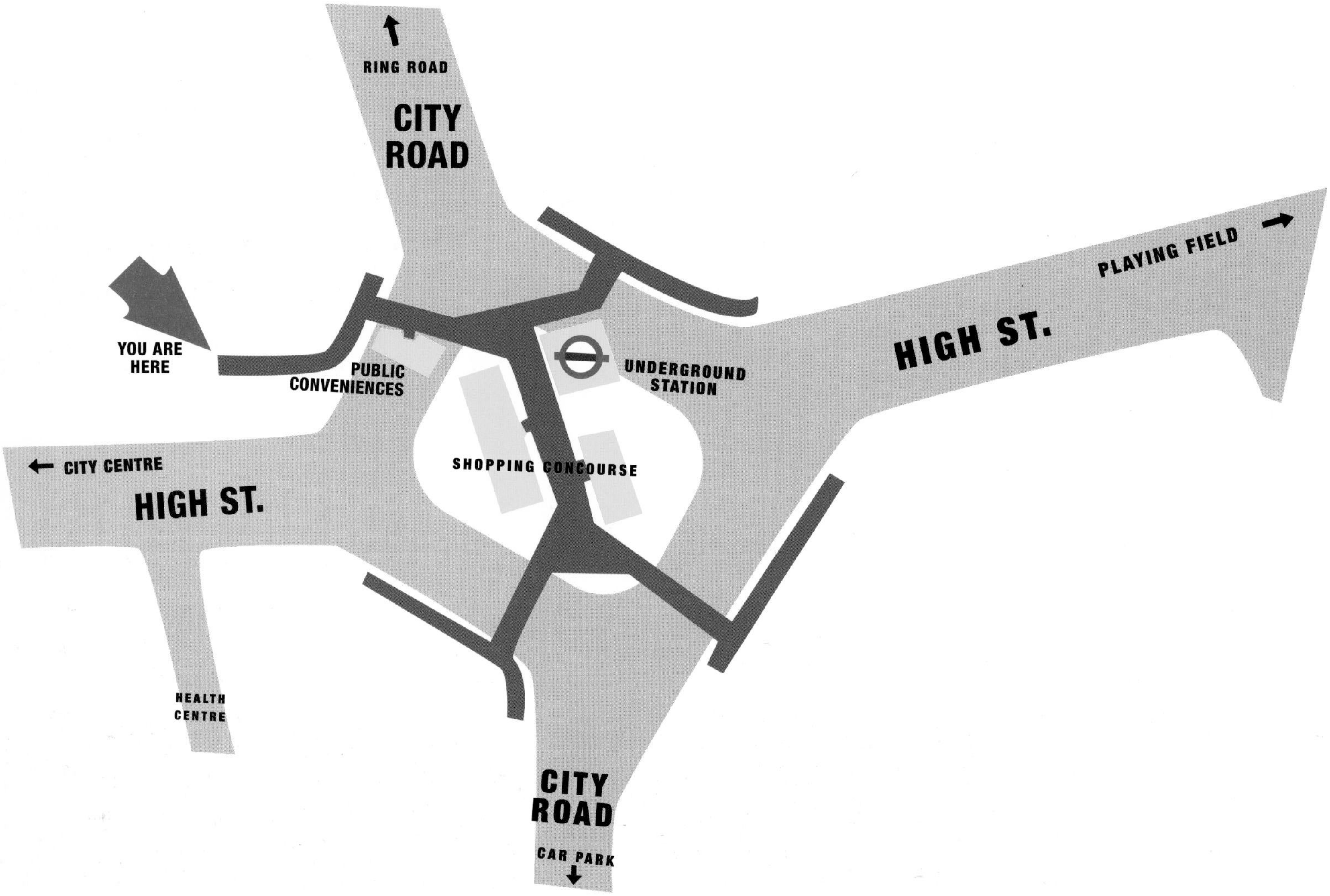

RING ROAD
CITY ROAD
YOU ARE HERE
PUBLIC CONVENIENCES
UNDERGROUND STATION
PLAYING FIELD
HIGH ST.
CITY CENTRE
HIGH ST.
SHOPPING CONCOURSE
HEALTH CENTRE
CITY ROAD
CAR PARK

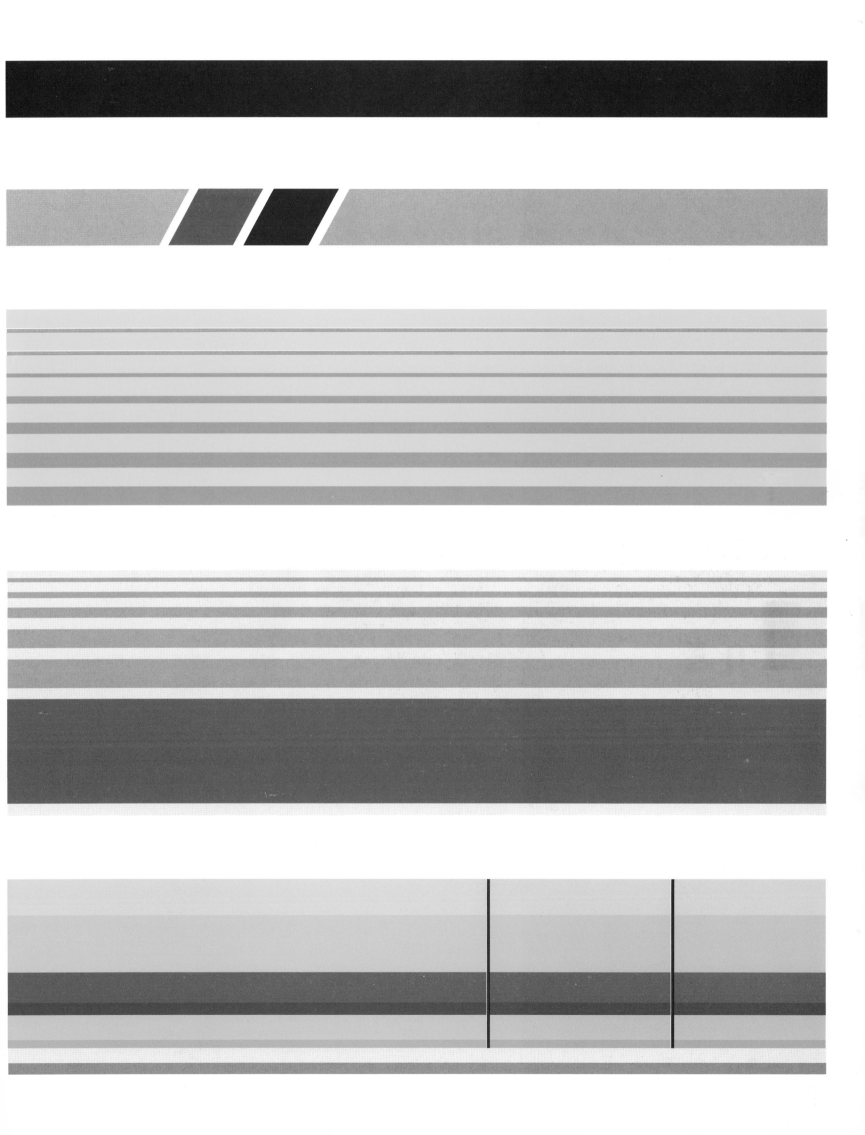

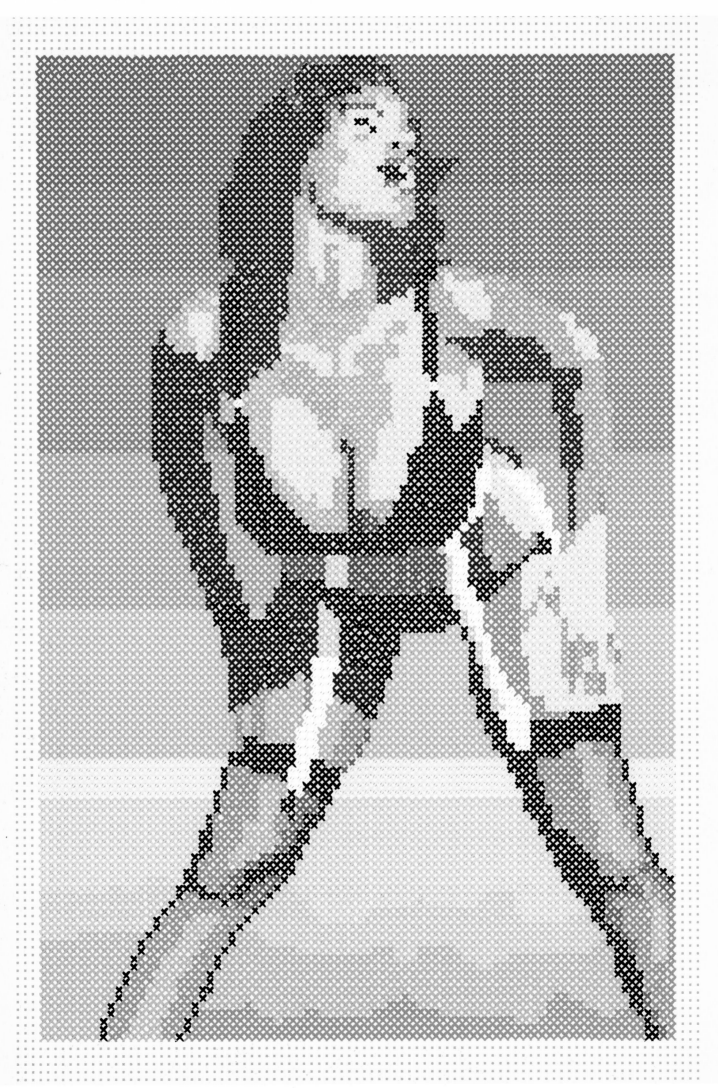

ST PETERSBURG, RUSSIA 'Chauki' *Colour Photographic Print* / KAI WIECHMANN - EAST PHOTOGRAPHIC T 0171 251 9003 page 40 / 41

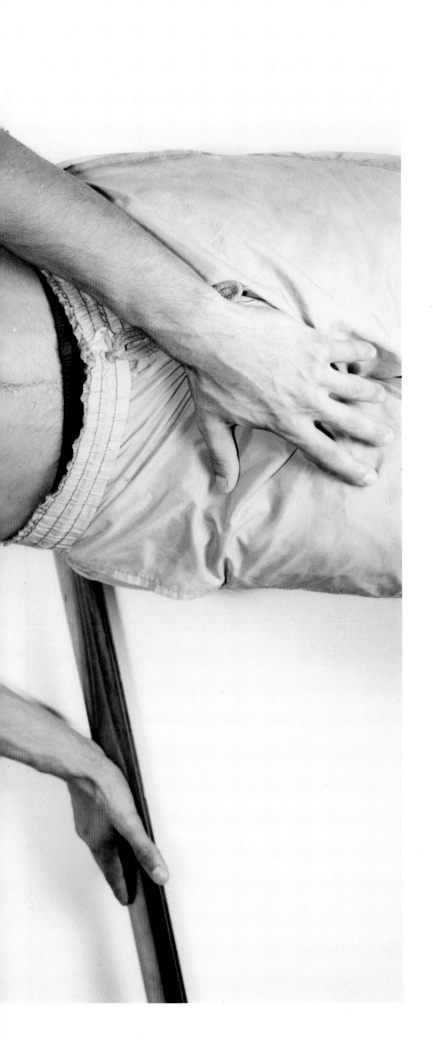

ST PETERSBURG, RUSSIA ·'Cash' *Colour Photographic Print* / KAI WIECHMANN - EAST PHOTOGRAPHIC T 0171 251 9003   page 42 / 43

ST PETERSBURG, RUSSIA *'Verex' Colour Photographic Print* / KAI WIECHMANN - EAST PHOTOGRAPHIC T 0171 251 9003   page 44 / 45

ST PETERSBURG, RUSSIA *'Addicted to Battle' Colour Photographic Print* / KAI WIECHMANN - EAST PHOTOGRAPHIC T 0171 251 9003   page 46 / 47

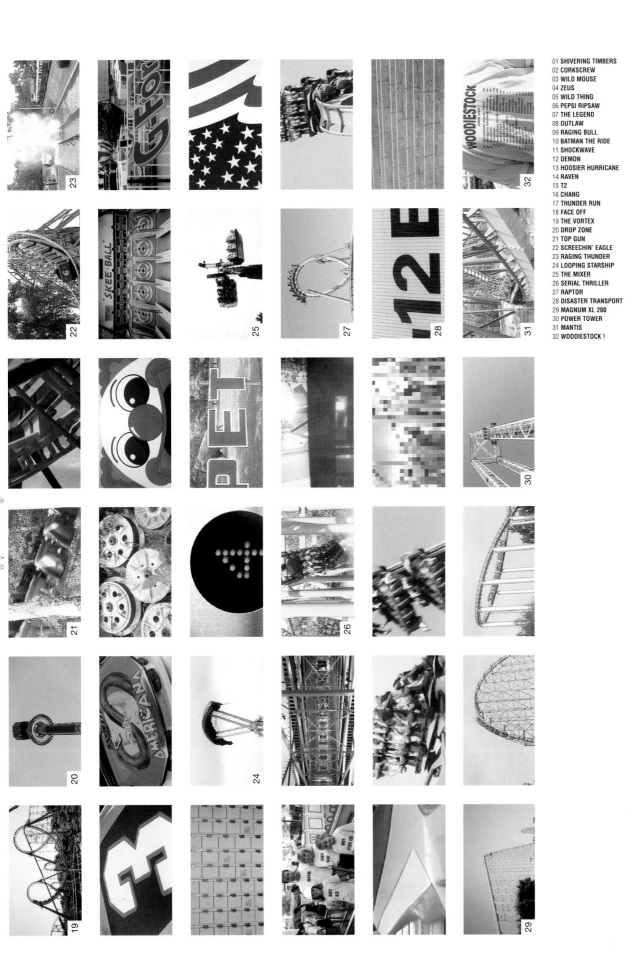

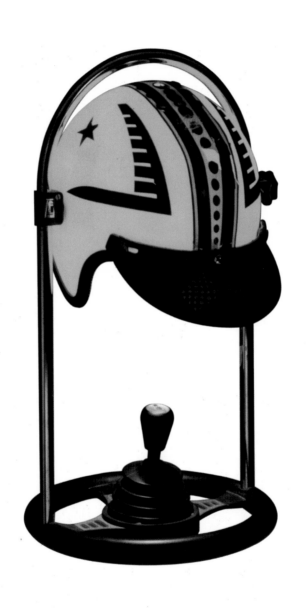

1234567890

ABCDEFGHIJ

KLMNOPQRS

TUVWXYZ

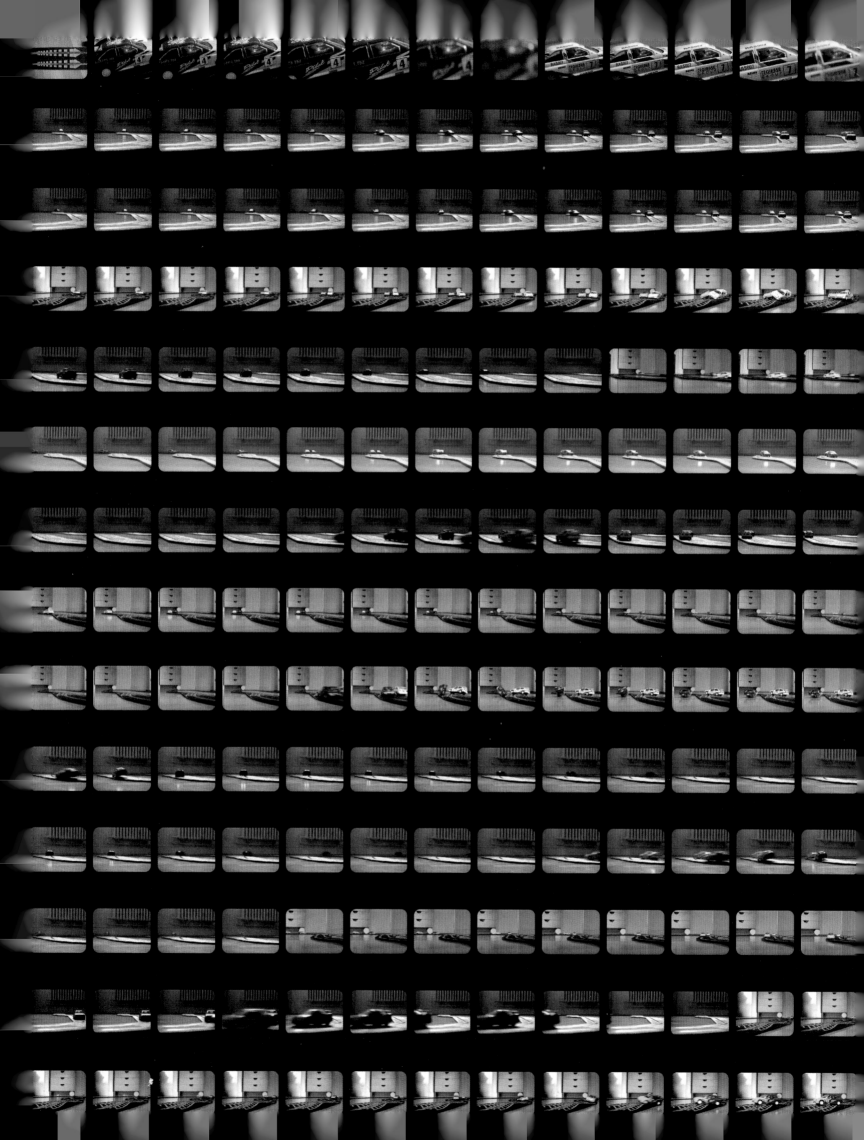

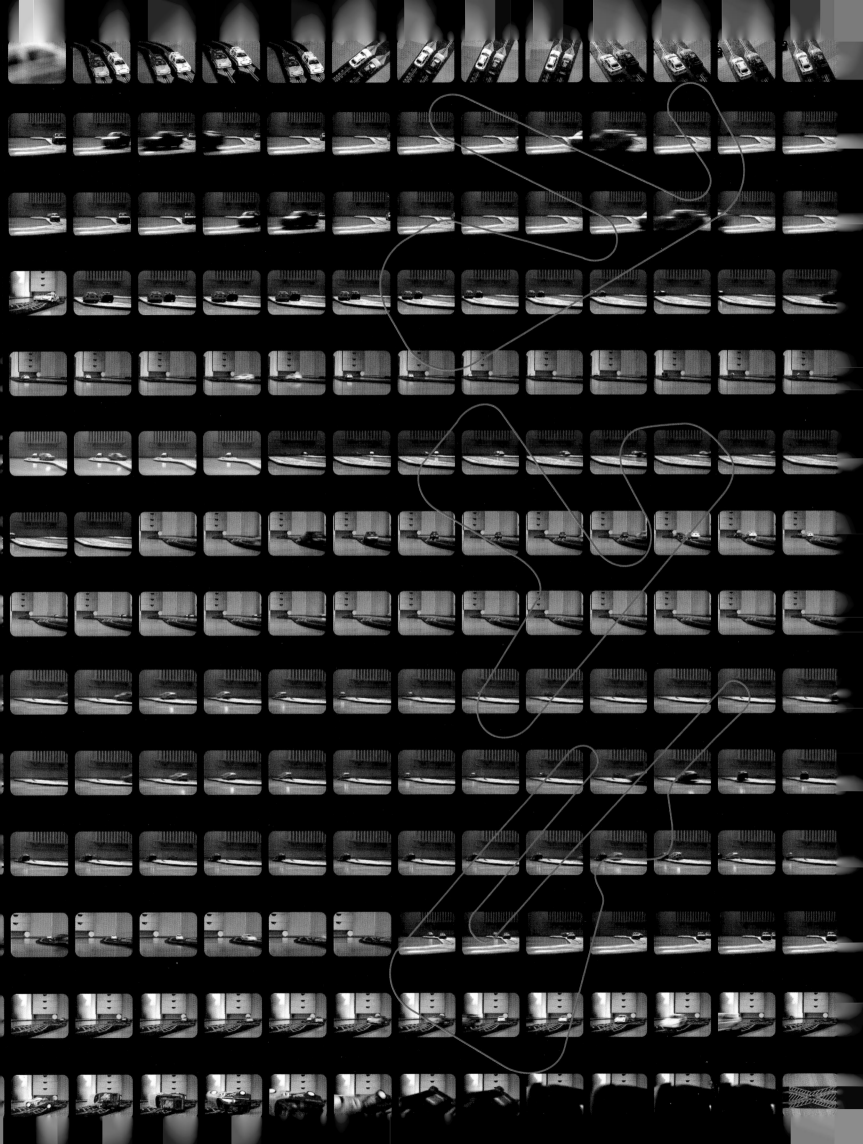

WARNING
MOTOR SPORT
CAN BE
DANGEROUS

DESPITE THE ORGANISERS TAKING ALL REASONABLE PRECAUTIONS
UNAVOIDABLE ACCIDENTS CAN HAPPEN IN RESPECT OF THESE YOU ARE
PRESENT AT YOUR OWN RISK

FUEL

BODY

LAP

POLE

SHAFT

GEAR

PARTS

PIT

CRANK

Discarded in a million old toy-cupboards nationwide lay the last heroes of speed. The seventies & eighties left a scrapheap of ridiculously absurd "Hot Wheels" - cranked up Corgi's, chassis bending Dinky's and fireball flame Matchbox models stretched the imagination to the limit. Playgrounds everywhere saw boasts of the biggest and bestest rear wheels or the most bonnet - bulging engine, but there was only one sure-fire test of the ultra-car…throwing it as hard as you could against the floor. This test would explain the condition and rarity of such models now. Absurdly enough, drag-racing uses the very same principles of playground supremacy. Machines that resemble both childlike sketches and the dreams of madman are tuned & groomed for years for 10 seconds of rubber-burning ecstacy - thrown against gravity itself. Below is a Dodge Challenger "Funny Car" named "Rambunctious" driven by the 1970 Texan Driver of the Year "Gentleman" Gene Snow - in this prestigious competition the biggest smoke cloud wins. Above, not so fast, but just as impressive (?) is Ed Pink's Wonder Wagon from 1973. *Men in drag eh ?…CT*

PUMP

PISTON

WRENCH

POSITION

LUBRICANT

SKID

RUBBER

HELMET

COIL

FINISH

THE ROOTS *Amhir / Colour Photograph /* PHIL KNOTT   page 66 / 67

THE ROOTS *Ambir / Colour Photograph /* PHIL KNOTT

The Roots are the best live hip hop band I'll ever see. Ahmir from The Roots lets me know a thing or two about them...Each member of the band let's see... We got... Wait a minute...Cut. Okay, describe each Roots member; describe yourself. How would your mother describe you? Thompson's being very sarcastic right now. Alright, let's see. Let's start with me... um... Everybody else that you've asked the question to, have they ever wound up describing themselves, or do they just say 'I don't know.'? Some say, 'Oh, I'm 5' 8"' and some will say 'Nah nah nah'. Alright, so will ?uestlove break the mould, or will he fall into the character of anyone else? Okay okay, I'll start with them first. Well as you see, first we have Kamal the keyboard player who's the youngest of the group; he's the baby. Um, let's see... Kamal the guy with the split personality, you can definitely see there are moments where he's definitely trying to vibe for position. Obviously the whole respect factor is an important thing for him. You know, there are some people who demand and command respect for their actions, but I've never seen anyone strive for it as much as he does. Usually when he's in front of people he's very guarded, this tough exterior comes to life, but then when he's in intimate situations with other people he's kind of like a kid, you know? One of the funniest moments with Kamal was when we were in Miami once, and we were in a mall. I'd never seen the stereotypical monkey with the organ, or a guy ask for change, but I saw it in this mall. These little kids were petting the monkey and everything, and Kamal sees and is (really loaded and excitable) "Oh man! Look at that monkey!" and he starts (Roadrunner sound) "Me me whoosh!!!". He just runs, pushing the kids out the way, "Hey! Oh man, you alright little girl?" It was like all these three year olds and six year olds just got pushed to the side, and he was like playing with the monkey and he wouldn't give the monkey up, and you know all the kids wanted to play with the monkey and he wouldn't let them, you know? So there are moments like that when he's a kid, then there are moments - like what you saw today with the monitor man (Kamal had a huge row with the monitor man during the sound check when wouldn't listen to Kamal asking for his monitor to be turned up) which I've not seen before - but I mean he'll loose it. I mean Tariq used to be like that, Tariq is older now - I think all of us used to be - I think everyone goes through that particular phase in their life. There's a point where you just get tired of it, I mean we're getting older now and there's no more time for that. So that's Kamal, sorry! Tariq. I mean Tariq's going through a transitional phase, I mean there were times about four or five years ago, when I don't know, we just had no hope. No, not saying we had no hope, but just like... oh yeah, there were times when he was more obnoxious to me than Kamal. But I guess just in getting older, this business can really humble your ass 'cos if you don't make it... Oh man! you're in for the shock of your life. Tariq's actually getting much more reserved and much more mature - that's how I vision Kamal when he's 25 years old. Hub is the dirty old man of the group, you know? I'm not gonna reveal Hub's age, but Hub always reminded me of...Have you ever seen the movie 'Diner'? No. Paul Reiser. He's a comedian. He was in 'My Two Dads'. There's this character in 'Diner' that Hub always reminds me of, this was Paul Reiser's character and he's...um... like...Hub is notorious for hinting at things he's after, but never saying. Like if you're drinking coffee and it's cold outside and you're really warm he'll say "Is that coffee you have there?", or "Oh, is that Tasters Choice or Gourmet Cinnamon?", or "Smells like cinnamon." You'll reply "Yeah", and he'll go "Oooh! Nothing like coffee to keep you warm huh?" Yeah yeah yeah... "So, um, how much did that coffee cost?" So, instead of just saying, "Can I have a sip of that coffee?" he'd be going round... like Hub's the hinter. That's what I'll say - Hub's the hinter! Rahzel. Rahzel is definitely the comedian of the group. Yeah, he's always cracking jokes, always playing the dozens... You know what playing the dozens is? Taking the piss. You know, he's the constant joker of the crew. And Malik B is the resident Houdini of the group, always pulling disappearing acts, and showing up when he's needed and amazing people at the same time. And er, I'm the ladies man! No! Ha ha ha ha! Let's see... how would you describe me? To some I'm an obnoxious asshole, to others I'm cool, and to

THE ROOTS Backstage / Colour Photograph / PHIL KNOTT

others I'm whatever. To others I'm a phone addict, to others I'm overrated, you know, to others I'm understated. I'm everything good and bad to them. **Can you tell me a little story about The Roots, including where you live and your funniest childhood memory?** Me personally? Yeah. So, I grew up in Philadelphia, Pennsylvania, January 20th 197- (Yawns and laughs) not to be mixed with 1970. But my funniest childhood memory? Two things ranked up there: 1, the first woman I was ever, ever in love with was Betty Rubble. My Mom breaking it to me was sorta a hard thing to take; I was three then. My second one was… how long has Sesame Street been out over here? **Probably 25 years.** Okay, what happened is - even to this day it haunts me -there's always something weird that scares the shit out of you when you're a kid… Actually there's two main things: they used to do that game on Sesame Street, like one of these kids is not like the other, whatever, but this time they decided to do an illustration of a starfish. There's three starfish and a crab, and it looked so damn eerie that to this day I can't watch Sesame Street without closing my eyes at the end of each skit, hoping that the starfish don't come up. So I'm like twenty - (Yawns again) years old, and I've never watched Sesame Street all the way through, like regularly, 'cos I know that one time it's just gonna come up and scare the shit out of me. My second childhood memory was the first week of school and the release of the Stevie Wonder album 'Songs In…', September 1976. **Hey, you're giving your age away now !** No! I didn't say what grade I was in though! I didn't say my first week, I said it was the first week of school… And my teacher, she pulled out the album cover - if you can recall it was just a bad oil painting of him, and ripples and whatever, and I thought it looked like he was drowning in a bunch of doughnuts - and I was just… 'ARRRRRGGGGHHHH!!!!!!!!!!' I did like the MacCaully Culkin Home Alone right, did the run through the wall type of thing and left my silhouette in there, that Bugs Bunny type of thing !! **How did you all meet? I'm afraid that might be a really boring question, is that alright?** No no, that's fine. Tariq and I… Black Thought and I met in High School at Philadelphia High School for Creative and Performing Arts, back in 1987. We started this group called 'Radioactivity'… Yeah it was corny but it didn't stick, and we became 'Black To The Future' a year later but it didn't stick, then we became 'Square Roots' in 1991 and it still didn't stick (because of legality), and we just became 'The Roots'… er… Then we started busking on the streets in 1992. Then in '93 we went to Germany with the help of a friend of ours, toured up and we were serving a six month sentence on Geffen Records! **You lived in London, am I right in thinking that?** Yes, you're very right. Um… we decided to escape from prison in 1994, when things weren't working out the way we wanted them to. So we took the last of our money and ran over here in 1994 and stayed. **Where abouts?** Kentish Town… Yeah (in Philly North London accent)… **Oh right!** We stayed in Kentish Town, right near Camden Market, yeah… Argh!!… Damn! I think in the peak, my Londinium accent was on point, but after not being here in such a long time it's hard to speak it. **Okay, if there was a cocktail entitled 'The Roots' what would be in it?** Right! First of all this cocktail would be one third hemp juice. It wouldn't contain… Um… It would be the only contradictory juice out. It would be one of those vegan health drinks, but it would be made of marijuana and it would still get endorsements from me and Rahzel, even though we're the only two members who don't smoke weed. **Oh! For most of our cover stars we ask them to come up with 10 commandments which revolve around the band.** Okay, number one: Thou shalt not let Ahmir use your telephone. Number two: Thou shalt not let Ahmir use your cellular phone. Number three: Thou shalt not let Ahmir use your hotel phone. Number four: Thou shalt not let Ahmir use his hotel phone. Thou shalt not let Ahmir into a business where there's a phone available. Thou shall not relinquish your phone card to Ahmir, or lend Ahmir money to get a phone card. Number seven: Thou shalt not let Ahmir fall in love with any woman outside a twenty-four block radius of his home because the phone bill repercussions will be deadly. Thou shalt not give Ahmir a stolen phone card number… what was that? Was that number nine? That was eight! Damn! can I do

two more? Thou shall hide all 'free long distance for three months' offerings from Ahmir... And our tenth and final entry: Thou shall cut off Ahmir's hands if he abuses your long distance. Thank you very much ladies and gentlemen. I think that's pretty cool you know! Yeah, so that's the basic rules right here. That's Ahmir's 10 Commandments. **Alright, tell us some Roots lingo. Lingo.** Actually a bunch of the colloquialism that we have been using, which you would deem 'dry' but, if they are 'dry' usage then they have maximum effect. In other words, like when you see a fine-ass girl, instead of doing the whole bug-eyed cartoon thing, we'll just say "Man, she is great." Like that is so bland. In other words, if you say "Wow! She is great! I mean great!!", with the calm emphasis that we put on that, it basically means that she was so great that we passed the point of excitement and we came right behind blandness. Like "She's just type great"... Ummm... 'beast'; when a woman is a beast, that means she's fine. "Yo, she is a 'beast!!'" Damn! I don't know if I should be revealing this joint but, er... 'Pydo' is P.Y.D.O, there's an acronym, that we use for - it's kind of hard being a politically correct group and saying shit like this, ai-ight f*** it I'm going to say it - "Pull Your Dick Out"... HA HA HA!!... Whenever you hear the term 'pydo' yelled around, that basically means... not that we're telling people to pull their dicks out!! Oh, let me see, we've recently picked up a French term used by our French Product Manager in MCA France, she just says "Not possible", but the way she says it is "Not pos-ee-bel." That's something we've been on lately. I know there's one more... Oh! The word we invented, "Illadelph", that's where we're from. I like this interview, I feel close to you now! Ah good! So go ahead. **Okay. What's the best thing you've discovered in the UK?** The best thing I discovered? My return ticket to the United States!... HA HA HA! Actually that's a miracle, because we're here for like two months, so for any on member of The Roots to have his return ticket coming back is practically a miracle! Actually, what's the best thing I've discovered? Um... Let me see... Here and Japan have a much broader record selection than anywhere in the United States, I mean they have it there but they take full advantage of it. I mean here, I could find James Brown's 'Payback' album for £25 which is reasonably expensive, but back in the States they be like "That's $300." So, that's what I'll say, good-ass records! Trace magazine; ooh! I'm sorry that's another magazine! That's **Okay.** Yeah and my ticket back to the US. **Alright, what about tour shenanigans, what have you been up to?** *(Ahmir grins and frowns at me.)* Oh, are you not gonna divulge? Uumm!... Next!... Tour shenanigans? Anything and everything has happened. Oh, **Okay. I want you to improvise an advert, but I don't know what product you'd want to use... we'll just say toothpaste for now.** Okay. (Puts on soft and sexy voice over style voice.) "Hi there, this is ?uestlove speaking and I would just like to say, have you ever had one of those 'not-so-fresh' feelings?"... HA HA HA HA HA HA!!... Wait a minute... Okay... "Well now you can ease your pain with Bell-Telephone. You know on those rainy nights when you're in your hotel in Barcelona and there's another episode of Roseanne on television, and you're tired of brushing up on your Spanish? There's nothing to do? Yeah! Just pick up the phone and dial 001 - the area code and the number of course - you know you'll be in heaven for an hour to an hour and fifteen minutes. Only to feel the anger of the starving band whose food money you ate up. And of course that will keep you more on your toes (or your feet), because when you're fighting five people at the same time you know you can't help but be more super-human, so to become more super-human I recommend everyone use Bell-Telephones. The preceding message does not necessarily reflect the use of Bell-Telephones or any of the employees of The Roots... Thank you." **Okay, last question: What next?** Things fall apart. Again.

The Roots is the wickedest Hip Hop band in the world.

OH MAN WE DON'T LIKE HIM HE DON'T PLAY ROCK

Prince Paul came to London a few weeks back and made a quick stop-over while promoting his 'Psychoanalysis (What Is It?)' album, labelled by many as "Hip Hop's First Comedy Album". I bumped into him at his recent Jazz Cafe gig, where we had a chat about stuff, and decided to do a proper interview over the phone when he'd got home and settled down a bit...

What have you been up to since we last met ? "Um... Let me see I went to California, to work on The Gravediggaz record. I did that... what else have I been doing?" **You said to me that you were going to be working on three albums.** "Yeah, yeah I've been doing that, and while I was out there I also met up with Dan The Automator and Octagon" **Excellent.** "We have a production group called The Good, The Bad and The Ugly they're primarily out in the West Coast, in San Francisco - and I kinda thought, I'd better get over there and start on the album we're working on." **We're hearing loads of things are coming out of San Francisco at the moment...**"Yeah, yeah it's a cool place, 'cos er... isn't Shadow from there?" **Yeah.** "He's actually going to be doing something with the album too. It's gonna be a real good album." **Can you tell me about the other members of The Gravediggaz?** About the other members of The Gravediggaz? Let me see, everybody knows The RZA, 'cos of the Wu-Tang. Also, we have Poetic - he goes by the name of The Grym Reaper - you might know him, he had a group called Too Poetic. What's the other? OH! I nearly forgot one of the main members of the group Fruitkwan; he goes by the name of The Gatekeeper. He was actually down with my group Stetsasonic, back in like the mid-to-late eighties." **Is the album going to be called *'Three Years On'* ?** "*'Three Years On'*? Ha ha ha! What are you talking about? The Gravediggaz one? I don't know what the record's gonna be called, to be honest with you we haven't even come up with the title! When I went out there I caught like the tale end of the making of the album. On the first Gravediggaz album, I did like a lot of stuff on it, but this one I kind of stepped back. The Rza did most of it. There are a bunch of tracks that I did this time - as far as production wise is concerned." **So you did a tour for Psychoanalysis. How long did that last?** "Oh yeah that was crazy! We did that for like a month, in February, it was like the 3rd to 26th or 27th... something like that. Yeah, that was cool. It was fun, but I'd never do it again. That was like a one show only out of character situation." **Yeah, everybody was really surprised !** "Ha ha ha ha! I don't know if surprised is good or bad but I'll just take it as okay!" **I was like trying to stand nearer the back every time.**"Ha ha ha!" **I think you were scaring everybody.** "Yeah it was like 'alright, but if you don't Ralphus will come and get you.' *(Impersonates Ralphus' perverted heavy breathing.)* I kinda liked that though! Yeah it was funny!" **I can laugh about it now, because you didn't pick me!** "Yeah now, because the fear isn't on!" **What's my next question? You've worked with so many people haven't you? Is there anyone you haven't worked with, and would really like to work with?** "Who I haven't worked with and I'd like to work with... Er maybe... I can tell you someone who I haven't worked with, and I am gonna work with, and that's Kool Keith. Yeah, 'cos I'm doing this record with Keith on Tommy Boy. Actually it's not really a record, it's more like writing and directing, which is gonna be totally ill. We're doing the soundtrack and everything. I'm probably getting another album out to show my talents, so that should be interesting. I think the title of the film will be 'Illegal Tender'. Hopefully I'll have an all star cast, but it won't star like the real popular people like Heavy D, Puff Daddy and Foxy Brown. It'll be a lot of underground and old skool people like Schooly D, Kool Keith, Dan The Automator... it's like people you know and people you don't know, like Chino XL and Xhibit... you know people who are there, but not really star-studded fame-types." **Can you tell us some predictions Hip Hop-wise to do with music and style?** "What, like I think where it's going to be heading?" **Yeah.** "Man, I don't know because if I did I'd be doing it right now! Ha ha ha! To tell you the truth, If I knew what the next thing was actually going to be Prince Paul would have it out by July. I don't know, from the looks it seems as though the underground is building up more, you know. A lot more kids are pressing up their own records, which is good, but it's sad because a lot of people don't have the outlets to get it to all the spots. Especially when I was out in Europe, there was a lot of the stuff I'd never heard of. And while I've been travelling around I was starting to realise there's a whole new underground scene. Like The Hieroglyphics crew coming back out, they're putting that out themselves, and it's like other little groups I've never heard before are coming out and they sound really good. I think it's rebelling against like the pop-rap." **Yeah, definitely 'cos London's got so much more. Like you'll go into a shop and Hip Hop'll be playing and it never used to be, and there are so many more clubs as well.** "Yeah, I remember when I was going to college in like the late 80's, and I was telling everybody like you know, 'cos it was a music college. And they were like, what music are you doing? And I'd do Hip Hop and they were like 'Urhh', like it was a sin. 'Rap?! Oh man!' And now the same school uses me as an advertisement so people'll go there. You know the same school that was like, 'Oh man we don't like him; he don't play any rock or any pop music.'" **Yeah, because fashion designers are getting really into it as well aren't they?** "Yeah, yeah yeah, right. You used to make it yourself, like Hip Hop style clothes and a Timberland or whatever, and now you get like Hip Hop clothes made for you. You know like the extra sag on the bottoms or a bit of graffiti writing on the shirt, I don't know! To be like that, that's really corny! It takes like all the brain power and all the thought power that you get to coming up with something, like prepackaging". **So, what did you think of London?** "I liked London, I just wish there was a little more sunshine!" So do we all! "I like it man. I didn't have chance to stay there long that time, because we were just like in and out! But, other times that I've travelled with like The Gravediggaz or Stets that was cool." **How old are you, if you don't mind me asking?** "Everybody wants to know how old I am! This is the answer I give: I'm not in my thirties... but I'll say this, I'm the same age as the Genius, but not as old as Kool Keith... so if anybody can figure that out!?" **Do you ever watch *The Simpsons*?** "Oh yeah! In fact I watched it yesterday!" **Excellent! because at the start you know where Bart Simpson is writing his lines on the chalkboard - what lines would you be writing if you were Bart Simpson?** "Ha ha ha! That's a funny question. What lines would I be writing? Man! What would people get at me for?... 'I will not bug out too much.'" **Who's your ideal date?** "My ideal date? That's a good question! Um *(goes quiet)*... I don't know! I don't have one. The reason why I don't, can't, have an ideal date is for the fact that everybody who I meet and I think is an ideal date isn't really, they're like an illusion or something. There's always something like fake about them. Like maybe they pick their nose or something. Like if I was to say Vanessa Williams or someone, you find out something you don't like, 'Urgh what's that thing above her eye? A growth or something.'" Urgh!?!! "...Or she spits when she talks. That's difficult to say. That's a good question!" **Aw! Because I was gonna ask where you would go should the opportunity arise?** "If I had an ideal date we would go to my house! Ha ha ha! Hey man, if I had an ideal date I may as well cut out the chase!" **Do you drink alcohol?** "No. Not at all."**Ah, 'cos I was going to ask what's your best cure for a hangover?** "No, you can't get me on that one! I really don't care for it that much. Except Baileys, and everyone told me that's a woman's drink. So, you know I can't drink that out in public!" **Do you like cooking at all?** "No, not really." **Oh, so where would you go to eat out?** "Where would I go to eat out? I'd eat at my Mom's house! See, because at my Mom's house I'm not limited to one type of food. There I can have some Italian, or some Hamburgers. If I went out anywhere, unless I went out to a diner I'd be totally limited." **Make up a cocktail and tell me about the ingredients and name?** "A cocktail, what would I have? I would have, one part Chocomilk. Chocomilk is like that chocolate drink from Holland. I like that man! I'd mix some milk with that just to make it a little thinner. And add a straw! I don't know if anyone would like that!" **What would you call it?** "I would call it... Oh let me see... ' A cup of surprise'." **'A cup of surprise'?!** "Yeah, I'd be surprised if anyone would drink it!" **What's the best movie you've seen lately?** "The best movie I've seen lately? Are you talking about a new movie?" **Well, it doesn't have to be !** "*Jerry Maguire. Jerry Maguire* and *The Beavis and Butthead Movie*." **So, what's good about those?** "Yo, *Jerry Maguire*'s touching, because if anybody has had a relationship, been in a similar situation, or felt like a certain way, like Tom Cruise felt in that situation, it made you kinda sad. Anything that strikes a nerve or pushes an emotion out of me. That's why I liked it, I kind of got into that. I was like, 'Oh man! I know how that is.' So that's how that was. Then *Beavis and Butthead* because I just think that they're the funniest cartoons out... except for *The Simpsons*." **Can you tell me three words, expressions or phrases that should be banned? Ones that really irritate you.** "Let me see, that really irritate me? Man, these are real good questions. Man, I would really have to sit down for a while. I guess of the top off my head, it's hate, because that's the cause of all types of wars, somebody getting beat up, any type of violence. There are a lot of words that would come into that: Racism. I don't know if I could block that all into one word, but that would be it. Let's see what other phrases are there that I wouldn't like: 'I don't understand you', 'I totally misunderstood', I don't mind people not really understanding me 100% , but to come to a conclusion, without really trying to understand me. You know like shit about me, like I messed up on whatever or make like prejudgments, I really don't get off on that at all. For people to sit down and to analyse something and make judgments." **Definitely.** "Okay my last one. Let me just say that I really don't like 'I'll bill you for that.'" Ha ha ha! "I don't like that at all." **Oh, that's all my questions is there anything you want to add?** "Anything I want to add?" **Yeah.** "Yeah, I got a few things, I need to sell my record. Please buy my Gravediggaz album, coming out in May or June. Please buy The Good, The Bad and The Ugly album, I'm not the ugly. With Shadow doing some production. Please buy my record, I don't know when it's coming out... sometime later this year, and look out for my movie. 'Cos it's gonna be... I'm gonna trend set this year, I just want everybody to know. I'll be coming out with something different, something ill and not necessarily trying to be different, just that my personality brings me that way. I'm definitely gonna come out with something great this year, and it's definitely gonna turn the industry round. And I hope not too many people bite, and if they do bite then I hope they do it really good. Let's see what... Oh Tommy Boy's re-releasing my *Psychoanalysis* album, so for a lot of people who couldn't buy it or find it." **Okay, I've got one last question and I think I already know the answer, ha ha ha!... Are you really a Prince?** "Am I really a Prince? Do you want a one word answer or a long answer?" **Quite a long answer would be good, if you can think of one!** "Okay, the first would be no, people just think I am! Ha Ha Ha!! And that's my answer !"

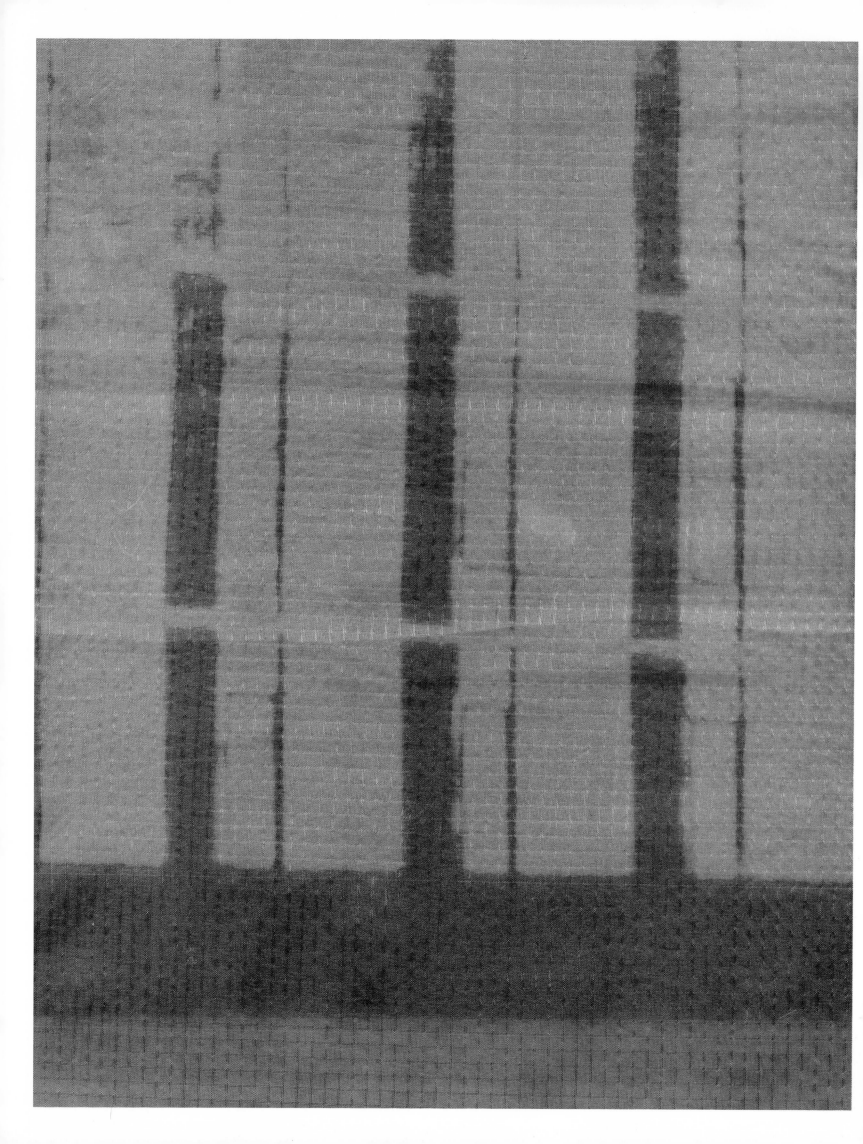

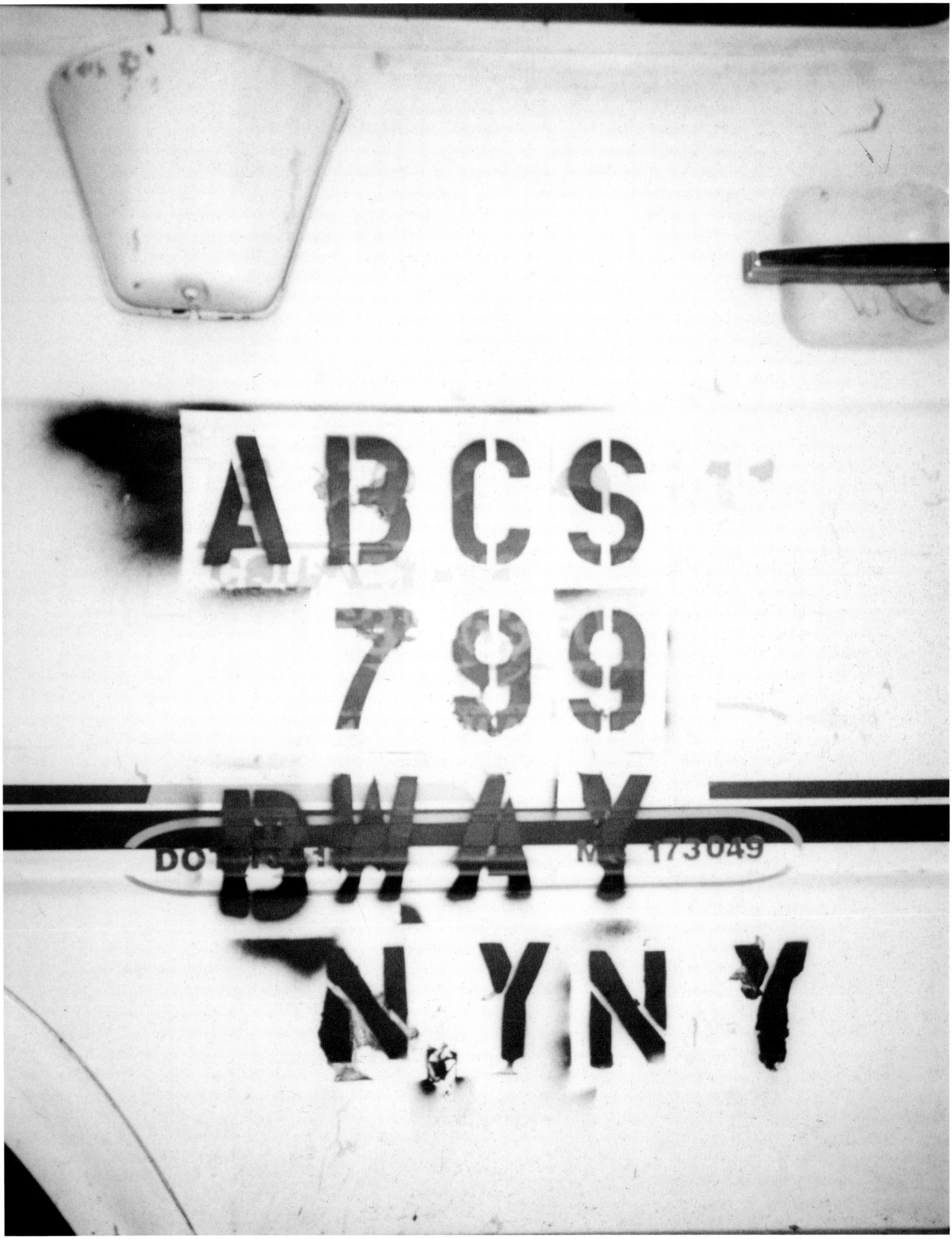
ABCS
799
BWAY
NYNY
173049

STAR DELIVERY
209 . KENEDY BL V
NB . N J .

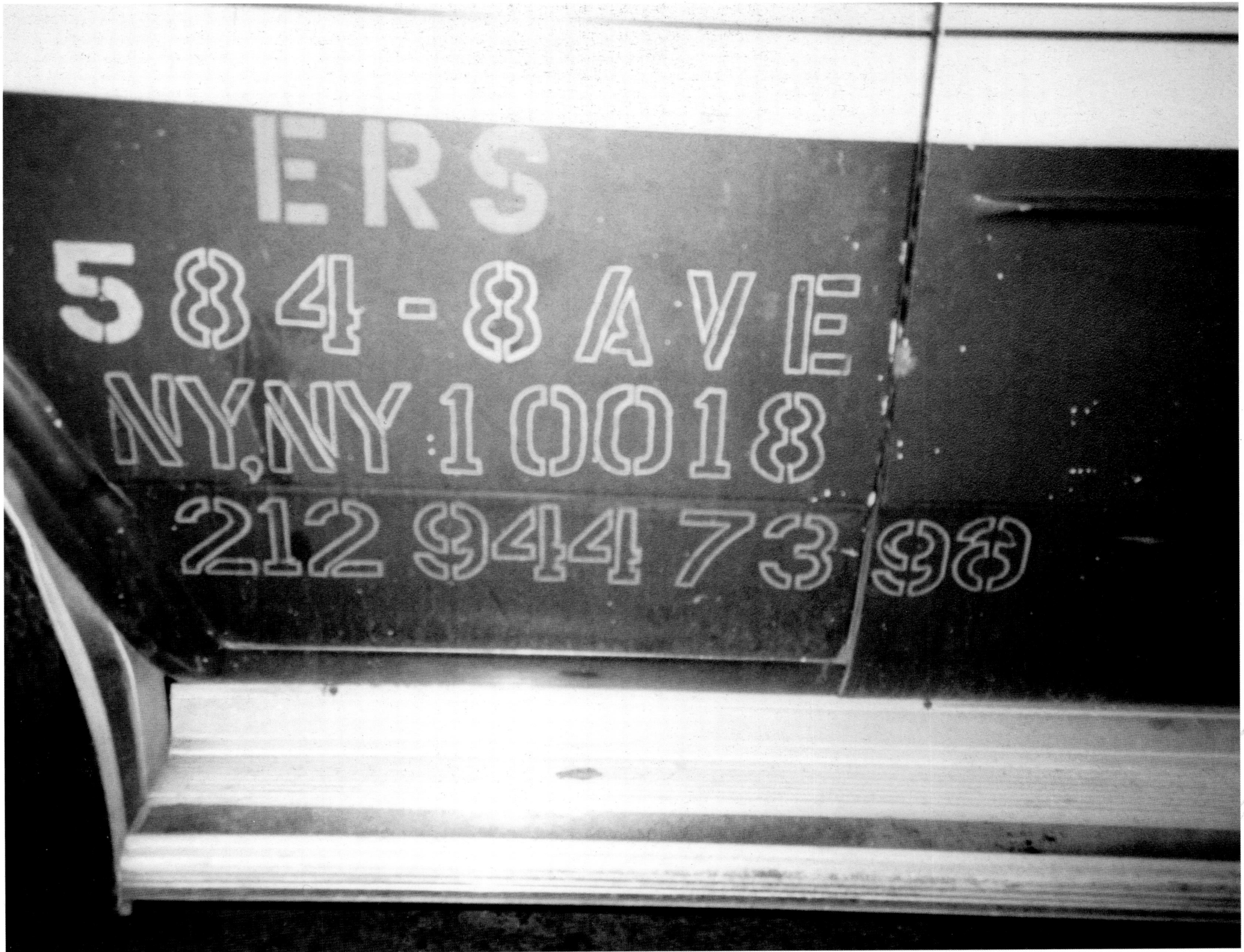
ERS
584-8 AVE
NY,NY 10018
212 944 7396

HELI TRUCKER INC

3445 30TH ST G/FL

NY NY 10010

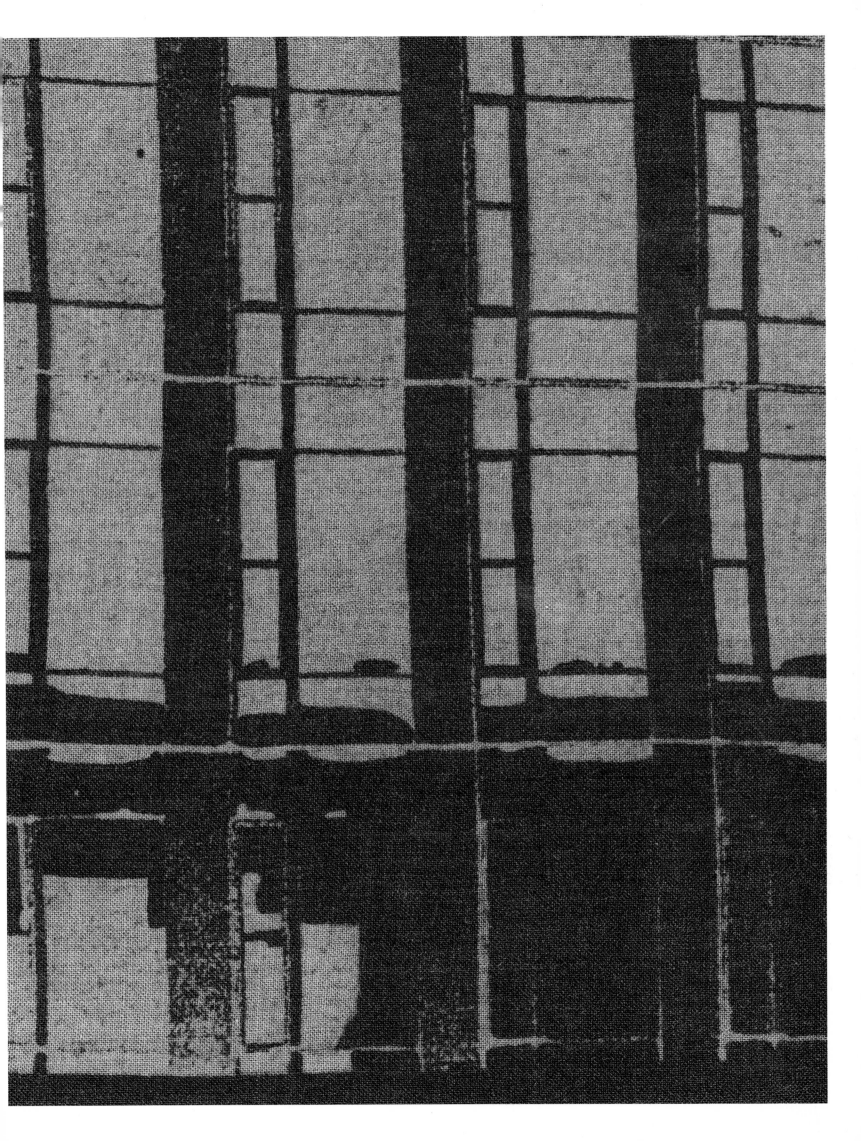

NEW YORK Skyscraper / *Scale Model* / MUSEUM OF MODERN ART, NEW YORK

Name: Malik Izaak Taylor aka Phife Dawg. Age: 29 on November 20th 1999. Occupation: MC. Residence: Atlanta, GA. How long did you live in New York? 23 years. Where's the best: a) area? I'd have to say Long Island, I couldn't really say what part of Long Island I like...Westbury, it's all good. Queens, the Jamaica Estates in Queens is one of the best areas to live. To live, I'd have to say around my way in St. Albany, and Manhattan to shop, you know what I'm saying? b) place to eat? Well one of my favourite places to eat is The Roty King in Long Island, but also a good place to eat would be...I'm a West Indian kinda sort so...Oh! Big Mama's in Manhattan, a soul food spot there...a very good place. c) place to socialise? Well it used to be The Tunnel, I know everybody still goes to The Tunnel but you have The Cheetah Club and there's this club that Q-Tip spins at on Thursday nights, it's pretty hot, I went there a couple of times. Me,personally Madison Square Gardens because I'm a big basketball fan, so The Knicks' games is where I like to socialise and at the actual NBA store in Manhattan, and the All Star Café. Just Manhattan period. It's the best place to socialise in New York City. d) place to party? Any hip hop spot in Manhattan. e) place to relax? There ain't no place to relax in Manhattan! I'd have to say Long Island or at home, ha! You know what I'm saying?! If you were asked to describe New York to someone who had never been before, what would you say? Dirty streets. A lot of congestion. If you go there in the summer it's very humid. The capital place for fashion, to shop for music, for clothes. The hip hop capital of the world, but it is fun, very crowded. People with bad attitudes. Describe New York in the: a) spring: That's the best time in New York, all the girls come out with the skirts, just looking mad good. Every bodies shopping, having fun, chillin'. The parties are amped. b) summer: Too damn hot! Just too hot! c) autumn: That's a nice time in New York too, everybody going back to school, doing there thing. d) winter: Too cold as far as I'm concerned, that's why I live in Georgia. Tell us your best experience in the city. This past year the Knicks made it to the finals. Doing shows. Most of the shows in New York City where always hot. Tell us your most memorable show, when, where and what went on. The most memorable show would have to be Washington, DC at Howard University's Home Coming. That was like November of '93 and 'Midnight' came out a week prior. We had a very good show then. We had this

Name: Freestyle Arsonists. Age: 24. Occupation: Hip Hop artist. Residence: Brooklyn, NY...Bushwick section. How long have you lived in New York? Since 1980. Where's the best: a) area? Manhattan b) place to eat? Any fun restaurant in the city (MARS 2112, JEKYLL & HYDE) c) place to socialise? Bars in the city, but I dont go to them. d) place to party? SOUNDFACTORY, WETLANDS, TUNNEL e) place to relax? Rockaway beach, Brighton beach, Manhattan beach. If you were asked to describe New York to someone who had never been before, what would you say? NY is fast paced, but full of life! despite what u hear about it, its good...I love NY and I will neva be able to live elsewhere. I believe. lots of fun and opportunities here. Describe New York in the: a) spring: Cars everywhere. people enjoying the weather, parks full. everyone hanging out in clubs. bars, etc...best time to be in NY! b) summer: Too hot ! Beaches full, everyone longing for air conditioning, mating season c) autumn: Nice time to be here, summer just over, and everyone gettin back into the work & school mode. d) winter: Too cold, people stayin indoors, runnin around to work, etc...Tell us your best experience in the city. Best experience in the city for me is the clubs back in the early 90's. They were soooo much fun back then, also, just hanging out playing pool, going bowling, central park, all the tourist spots & movies.

place called the DC Armory and what went on was - we was rockin' so bad that people started pushing the barricades and falling over each other a little bit. girls running up on stage trying to touch Q-Tip. It was cool, it was real cool, but I got kind of scared for the people for a moment because a couple of people got trampled, but it didn't get out of hand 'cos we fixed that in a minute. So that was one of the most memorable shows. Oh! Another show was in California in like KMDO, which is a station in the Oakland San Francisco Bay Area, they have a summer jam every summer and there had to be at least ten thousand to fifteen thousand people there and we just tore it down! This was when 'Low End' was out. We just killed it ! I remember that very well. And the whole Lolla-polooza experience, that was very good. I didn't want to be there at first, but I left saying 'Yo! I'd do this again!' That was good, thanks to the Beastie Boys for putting us on. You know what I'm saying, so that was dope.

Name: Bobbito. Age: Timeless. Occupation: DJ, MC, host, entrepeneur, (Fondle 'Em Records, Bobbito's Footwork - NY + Philly stores) Residence: NY. Where's the best: a) area? Upper West Side. b) place to eat? Il Bagato 2nd St bet Ave A & B. c) place to socialise? Any basketball playground. d) place to party? House parties in Brooklyn. e) place to relax? Anywhere outside the five boroughs. If you were asked to describe New York to someone who had never been before, what would you say? Ice cream / assorted sobet flavours. Describe New York in the: a) spring: Slipping out of darkness. b) summer: Witness the most beautiful array of people assembled in the world. Lots of outdoor music. c) autumn. Find a woman, winter is long. d) winter. Everyone looks like a hardrock, accessories you've never imagined being progressive fashion. Tell us your best experience in the city. '94 Rock Steady Crew Anniversary. What record sums up New York in the following situations: a) Getting ready to go to a party. Stevie Wonder 'Do I Do' b) Travelling round town. Kool G Rap 'Streets of NY' c) and two of your own choice. Ella Fitzgerald 'Autumn in NY' Kool & The Gang 'Give It Up'.

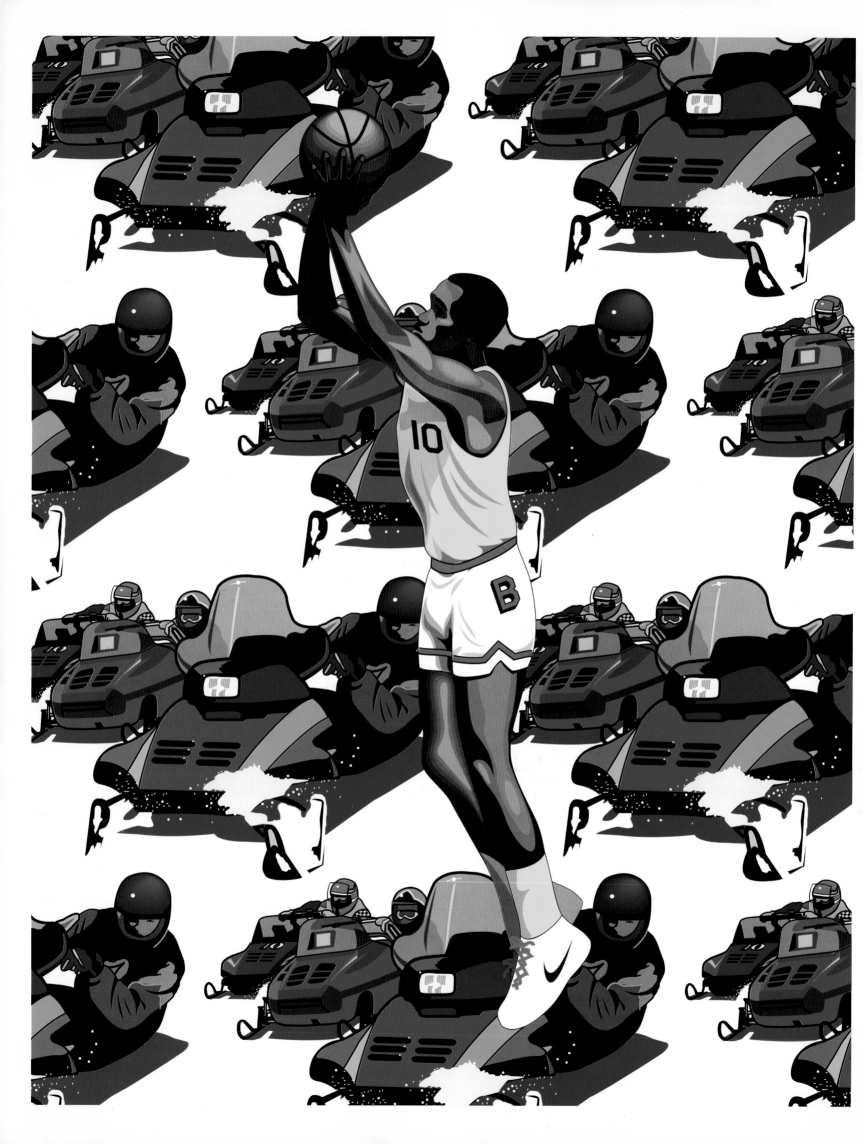

You'll probably know Afu-Ru from one of the following places…

…straight out of the Gang Starr camp…

...sidekick to none-other than Jeru the Damaja...

...now Afu-ra is sepping on stage on his own with a whole host of works...

...blag presents one of his many talents...Tae Kwon Do...

QUICKER THAN THE HUMAN EYE...

...no better way to compliment this action section...

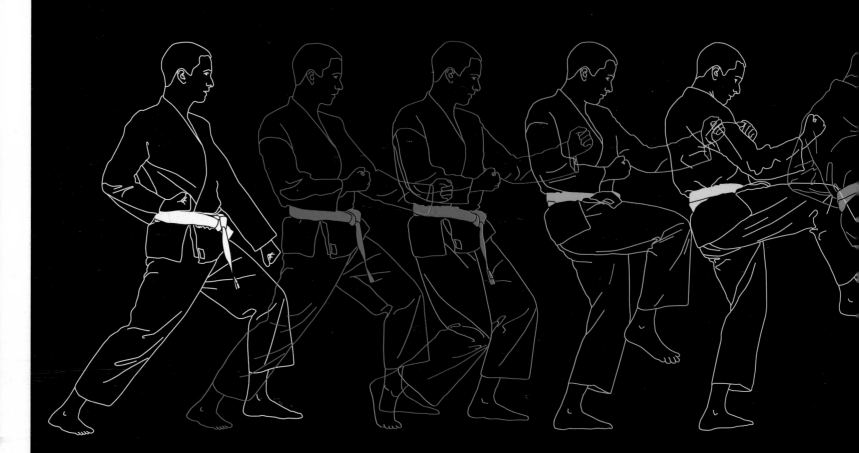

PHAI

ROUT
BOUT

THE PHARCYDE / *Colour Photograph* / SARAH EDWARDS / *Interview* / SALLY EDWARDS

LA's finest hip hop outfit, The Pharcyde, who not only MC, harmonise, dance and produce beats for a living, now have to get to grips with a blag interview. Outside a venue in London they pose for Sarah to take some photographs, then make themselves comfy on a fence for the tape to roll and the answers to flow. First up is the all important introductions...

Yo! My name is Bootie Brown from The Pharcyde. Wussup, my name is Imani from The Pharcyde. Slim...Kid. Right, describe yourselves. Well, my name is Bootie Brown. I'm about 5' 9", 151lb, brown skin. You know hip-hop enthusiast. **Imani:** 5' 10", very brown skin, locks, nose ring, I like to get high everyday. I really love females, I'm not gay, I don't have no problem with gay people. I'm cool. I'm into metaphysics. I'm into the other side you know what I'm saying? I really like booties, and I like to do shows in England...Hip Hop! Yeah! And I like Hip Hop. **Slim Kid:** Hi! Yeah, well you know...I'm tall, I'm slim, I'm a Libra, I'm a ladies man, I'm a man for the ladies. You know I eat my vegetables, I mean what mo' can I say? Ha ha. Tell us a short story of The Pharcyde, including your home and area, and your mums. **Bootie Brown:** These are like personal. **Imani:** Arrrghh! Ha Ha! Well this is how it is, but you don't have to answer if you don't want to. **Boootie Brown:** No, it's okay, what d'you want me to start with, my mum or...? Oh, it's up to you. **Bootie Brown:** Hhmm...Well I was born in Pasadena. It's like I guess you would call it a suburb, you know what I'm saying? It's mostly like residential, not really like too much of a city type area, more like residential houses type place. So I'm a suburban kid, you know what I'm saying, my mamma was a suburban mum you know, 'Come home son before the street lights come on' and all that. So that's how I was...Yep! Um...You look like a go-go dancer. *(Imani's stepped inside one of those cages you transport goods to a grocery store in - he's shut himself in, and he's looking all proud of himself!)* **Everyone:** HA HA HA HA HA! **Bootie Brown gets back on track:** So, yeah I mean, I don't know. The Pharcyde...How we started. We just started doing our thing. We got tired of dancin', you know what I'm saying? We'd been dancing, and it was like 'Yo man, we gotta quit this shit. We gotta start taking charge of what we wanna do.' So we said 'Enough of the dancin'. Let's be the rappers,' and that's how it started moulding up to the whole thing. Finish this sentence: The Pharcyde are... **Imani:** Individuals. That's all I can say, you know what I'm saying? We're all different, but we're kind of alike in certain ways, you know? Like you're twins, you know what I'm saying, you guys are alike but...you know what I'm saying, you're different. **Slim Kid:** The Pharcyde are S.T.U.V.W.X.Y.Z. Tell us what we don't know about you. **Slim Kid:** You know everything. **Bootie Brown:** The size of my... **Imani:** The size of my cock! **Slim Kid:** Hahahahaha! The size of my thing! **Bootie Brown:** ARRGH HAHA-HAHA! There's a lot of things you don't know, and I wouldn't wanna tell you, you know what I'm saying? You're not supposed to share all your information. That would be bad 'cos you know if I was a drug dealer...**Slim Kid:** What sign are you? I'm a Leo. **Imani** *(changing the subject now):* This girl said to us that she didn't think we were very nice when she saw us on stage, are we not nice? Do we not look nice? No, you're nice. *Imani laughs.* **Slim Kid:** The Pharcyde are nice. Okay, who do

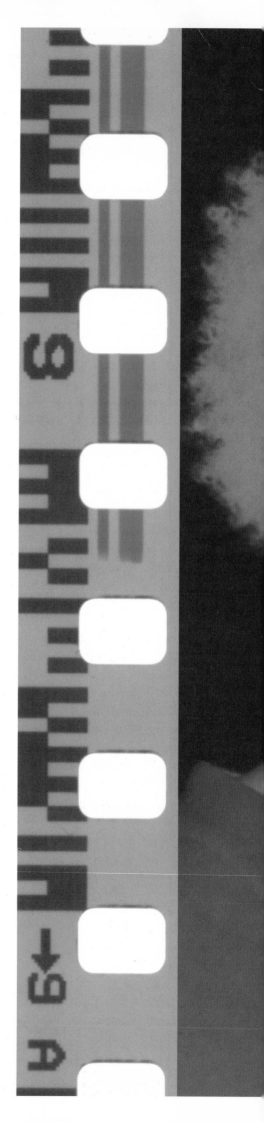

Imani

you love? **Imani:** I love the Universe and the Cosmos. **Bootie Brown:** I love Taci. **Slim Kid:** Heh heh, for real? Um I love my girls. Tell us what you think of London? **Imani:** I think it's cold. **Bootie Brown:** Oh, it's cool right now. I think this is the first time I've ever been here and the sun is actually out. It's cool, you know what I'm saying? It has it's different flavours. It's kinda like New York with it's mixing of a lot of cultures, but then it's totally different because it has a total different culture mixture than New York has.

Who would you most like to play Twister with? **Slim Kid:** Twister? You guys on your birthday! **Bootie Brown:** HA HA HA HA! **Imani:** You guys. WOOOOOH! *(With lots of claps.)* **Slim Kid:** Twister with the twins! Right, is there any particular sports you partake in? **SlimKid:** Sports? Butt slappin'! HA HA! **Imani:** Got the gold medal in that in '88! **Bootie Brown:** I got a silver in rollin' blunts. Ha ha ha! Do we? No, we look at sports. We been lookin' at the Olympics since we been out here. **Imani:** Computer games. **Bootie Brown:** Yeah I would like to play Basketball, but hey! I can't. **Imani:** Hey! Who would you most like to play Twister with? Who would I? Oh, I don't know. **Bootie Brown:** Don't know? **Imani** *(asks Sarah):* How about you? **Sarah** *(laughing back at Imani):* Oh definitely you, ha ha ha! **Bootie Brown:** She said definitely you! WOOH!

Alright, when did you last get involved in a fight? **Imani:** Yesterday this punk-ass bull tried to step to me, talk some bullshit I just bombed him mother f***er! BOMB! **Bootie Brown:** I had to slap my woman, you know what I'm saying? Some OJ type shit, you know what I'm saying? KShh KShh KShh!!! No, I had to grab her you know what I'm saying? All that bullshit. Naw…I'm not a violent person. We all about love, peace and happiness. **Slim Kid** *(singing):* I love you, you love me. **Bootie Brown:** There's no reason for me to fight. I'm a lover not a fighter! HAHAHA! **Slim Kid** *(asking Bootie Brown):* What feels better? Punches or breasts?! **Imani:** Or pelvic thrusts?! HAHAHA! **Bootie Brown:** I don't know. **Slim Kid:** Punching or pushing?!! **Bootie Brown:** Some people's into both. Changing the subject, what do you cook best? **Bootie Brown:** Mushroom tea, ha ha ha know what I'm saying? Ha ha ha!!! No, what do I cook? I know how to make some bomb-fish-taccos, on the real, I'm telling you. So you're not a vegetarian then? **Bootie Brown:** Oh, I eat fish that's about it. I don't eat nothing too much else; baked potatoes. **SlimKid:** You're talking Dinosaur when you say vegetarian. **All:** HAHA!!! **Bootie:** You a vegetarian? All the way? Like you don't drink milk? Oh no. No, I'm not a vegan, I'm a vegetarian. **Bootie Brown:** Okay, gotcha. **Imani and Slim Kid** *(In 'I get it' style):* Oh?! **Bootie Brown:** You just eat leaves and fruit. **Imani:** Nuts and Berries? You don't eat nuts do you? It takes five years off your life. Oh, I'll stop then. *(In deadpan style)* Ha ha ha ha ha !!! Make up a cocktail, ingredients and name. **Slim Kid:** Oh a cocktail? Mmmmm. **Bootie:** Bailiac. What's that? **Bootie Brown** *(holds out one hand):* Ice. *(Then the other):* Baileys, Hennessy. **Slim Kid:** And a glass. **Bootie Brown:** You need two-thirds of Baileys, one third of Hennessy, then shake very well. **SlimKid:** Then drink to your heart's content. **Bootie Brown:** Bailliac for the Brainiac. Sex on the beach, Sex on the roof. **SlimKid:** Sex on my roof! **Imani:** Sex on the waterbed. **SlimKid:** Sex!

If you had your own film, who would star in it with you and what would it be about? **Bootie Brown:** Who would star in it with me?

Imani: They would star in it with me, and it would be called The Pharcyde. **SlimKid:** Starring him with me, and me with him. **Bootie Brown:** It would have Robert De Niro in, and we'd call our shit; 'Thugs!' Hahaha! What happens in it then? **Bootie Brown:** Some gansta shit. **Slim Kid:** Mob shit. **Bootie Brown:** We'll get Robert De Niro to play Esce from Downtown Los Angeles, you know what I'm saying? He's in jail and he's calling the shots. We have a gang of people, doing a gang of stuff. **Slim Kid:** Then we just go "Yo, f*** you DeNiro. We're not listening to you no more. We ain't taking your cars no more. You know what I'm saying? From the jailhouse, and we're gonna start running this shit ourselves. Then he's gonna get out, and we're not gonna know about it and he's gonna f*** us up. **Imani asks me:** If you could be any animal, what would you be? **Bootie Brown:** You would be a cat! I was gonna say I'd be a lion. **Slim Kid** *(In my accent):* A lion? **Bootie Brown:** You're only saying that 'cos you're a Leo! **Imani:** A Leo, yeah alright! **Bootie Brown:** You're still in the cat class! Why, what would you be? **Imani:** I would be a unicorn. **Slim Kid:** I would be a Teracajacsauras. **Bootie Brown:** A Teracajacsauras? Ha ha ha!! I am an animal, araurrraaagh!" *(That's supposed to read like a roar)* If you had your own TV show, what would it be like? **Slim Kid:** It would be a porno. Ha ha ha! Ha ha ha! Everybody says that! **Imani:** It would be about sex, drugs, violence and music. I would have the top rated show on night-time TV. **Bootie Brown:** I would do a talk show. I wanna be like David Letterman, you know interview some real people, like people off the streets. Ray Ray, ha! 'Yo Ray Ray, what's going on in your life?' **Imani being Ray Ray:** 'I had a 40 this mo'ning, a 40 this mo'ning.' **Slim Kid:** I would do Three's Company, but I would serve my room mates! The Pharcyde have world domination, how's it run? **Bootie Brown:** I'd like to bomb out. I'm gonna make me a space ship, and you guys can keep it! I'll have a space ship and live underground in Mars and live on some dope shit.

You're The President, what's your slogan? **Slim Kid:** Get a job! Ha ha! **Imani:** Love, Peace and Happiness. **Bootie Brown:** You are what you eat. Tell us The Pharcyde's version of The 10 Commandments. **Imani:** Thou shall not kill. Thou shall not steal. Thou shall not talk shit about my Mama. Thou shall not talk shit about my family, or I'll have to kill you. Thou shall not talk shit about me rolling blunts, because I do what I wanna do. Thou shall not say anything about The Pharcyde that's derogatory. Thou shall not speak The Pharcyde's name in vein. Thou shall not serve my homie's girl. Thou shall not f*** my homie's wife. **Slim Kid:** Yo! Thou shall get our money from our record company, or thou shall get their arse whooped. Tell us some of your lingo. **Slim Kid:** Some lingo? Yeah. **Imani:** No! They gonna take it back to their hood. **Bootie Brown:** Skeets is our vocabulary word for the day. **Slim Kid:** And today's word boys and girls is: Skeets. How would you spell that Mr.Robinson? **Bootie Brown:** I'd spell that S.K.eets. Monetary, cash, buckola, loot, dollar dollar bill ya'll. *Imani takes control of the tape recorder,* Fat Lip is in the hospital having Lip surgery, I repeat Fat Lip is in the hospital having Lip Surgery. It has not been confirmed yet whether it is an increase or decrease in size. Thank you!

Thank you!

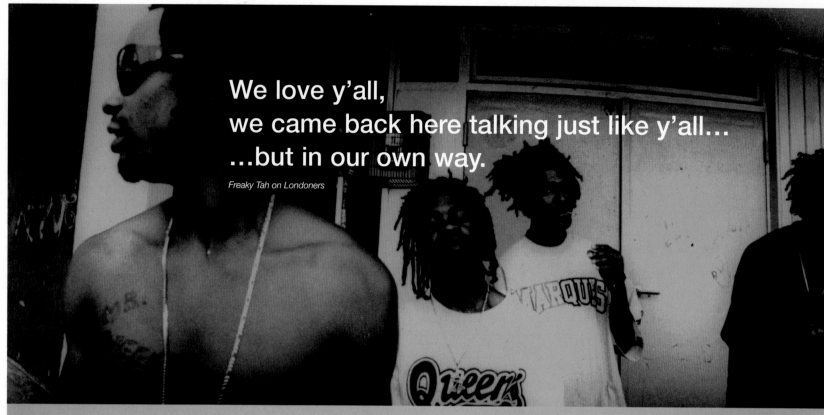

We love y'all,
we came back here talking just like y'all…
…but in our own way.

Freaky Tah on Londoners

LOST&

'YYYEEEAAAHHH…L.O.S.T…B.O.Y.Z… *Some people ask: 'Yo what is the Lost Boyz man? The Lost Boyz is us: Mr Cheeks, Freaky Tah, Pretty Lou, Spigg Nice…Recognise Lost Boyz man, East Coast man, shout out to the world man! We're gonna start the revolution man!' - Lost Boyz, intro to 'Legal Drug Money'.*

Summer…summer time…it's summer time in New York City and it's boiling hot. We're here to meet The Lost Boyz. That's right we finally got the interview we've been wanting for over a year, by coming here ourselves! Stepping into the room, we are greeted by three of the four blunt-loving members of the LB Fam. (Fam meaning Family.) There's DJ Spigg Nice sitting in the centre, to his right Pretty Lou, who's just finished playing on a PlayStation. Then there's Freaky Tah who kind of sings when he talks, and grins like he's got something up his sleeve. Someone does a high pitched impression of Cheeks …

Where is he? **Tah:** He's taking care of business *(The Lost Boyz are checking through the*

pages of blag #10, and getting carried away with the prospect of buying the Dragster bikes we featured last time around.) **Tah:** So, wass the deal? Well, I want you to describe yourselves in three words? **Tah:** One shot dealers. Okay, so are you enjoying life as The Lost Boyz? **Lou:** No doubt, I'm enjoying life as…**Tah:**…Our life is lost. **Lou:**…We live the Lost Boyz life. **Tah:** That's the name of our lifestyle. That's not the name of our crew or our gang, we're not a crew or a gang, we're a family, you know what I'm saying? That's why we section ourselves as The LB Fam, know what I mean? Whoever or whatever, the other Lost Boyz are doing…we ain't out there to tell them or anyone what to do. Everyone living their lives and is taking care of their business. **Is it hectic or chaotic? Tah:** It all depends, if there is jealousy out there, if they'll don't like you. There's a lot of police out there who take their jobs to extremes. You know what I'm saying? To make you look little, you know what I'm saying? It's real, life is what it is, you know. You got to know how to deal with it. **Lou:** Yeah. **Tah:** You've got to know how to play the game. How would you describe the Lost

Boyz music to someone who'd never heard it at all? **Lou:** It's a feelin'. You could say it's euphoric. You could say it's many different things you know. It's just an ill feelin'. **Spigg:** It's an experience. It's an understanding. Describe your neighbourhood. Have you got any infamous neighbours or locals? **Lou:** Yeah. **Spigg:** There's famous cats from around our way. Honest is from around our way. Who else? **Tah:** Run DMC, Onyx… all the old skool niggas… **Lou:** *(clicking his fingers)* I'm tryin' to think of… What's his name?…Y'all know!…Oh what's his name? One of them cats from…um…**Tah:** Full Force? **Lou:** No no no *(frantically clicking his fingers)*…You know the cat…He lived across the street from…Oh he used to be down with them *(busts into rhyme)*…Fruitkwan and my DJ Paul. **Tah:** Oh! Stetsasonic! **Lou:** Yeah, one of them cats used to live around my way, Organized Konfusion too. Tah: Now we're older we see the game's deep and we ain't learning from them, but we didn't even know they was in the game. We have a lot of talent around our way. **Lou:** And there's still more coming. Alright can you make up a cocktail ingredients and

This is dedicated to the memory of Freaky Tah, who was shot tragically in March 1999. Rest In Peace Freaky Tah. We'll miss you.

FOUND

name? **Spigg:** Hennessy, Guiness. Okay: Tequil **Tah:** Nah! Tequila! That's a side order. **Lou:** Hey I like that man, I like that. **Tah:** Hennessy, Jack, Tangueray, you know that's if you ain' t drinking the brown stuff. **Spigg:** Becks, Guiness, Red Stripe. **Tah:** St Ives, occasionally. That's about it. We smoke a lot of weed; we smoke more weed than we drink. Can you tell us five things that make a really good night out? **Lou:** Cheeba...Woooh!...Liquor... Wooh!...**Lou and Tah:** Condoms...Wooh! **Tah:** Two ass...Wooh! *(Everyone cracks up and starts clapping.)* **Lou:** Good answer! **Tah:** Carries on...and two titties: T and A. **Lou:** And music; Oh god! **Tah:** Cheebas and liquors, and condoms and two women. *(They all get very excited and shout over each other about go-go music.)* So, you all used to work at JFK Airport didn't you? Can you tell us funny stories about that? **All:** No doubt. **Spigg:** We seen a lot of funny people. **Tah:** The funniest thing about working at JFK was that you bought an outfit and the money's gone. You get to go to school fresh for two days. **Lou:** And you made club money. **Tah:** You get your weed, you get your joint on, you

get your outfit and tomorrow you'd be like this *(Holds out empty hands and looks disappointed)*… That's part of life. You got to keep goin'. You never stop and if that's what it takes to go get it, go get it. **So that was my last question, that was quick wannit? Tah:** Did you hear that she said 'wannit'! **Spigg:** That's not it, you got more things to say than that? **Alright so talk away then. Tell us about your time in London? Lou:** We had a ball in London. We were out at so many places, I'm surprised you didn't run into us in no club in London. **Spigg:** We stayed in London and I got the trains too. I got three different types of trains, like the old trains, then I got in the more advanced trains - so that was alright! - then it was the WOOAH FUTURISTIC. Ha ha ha! **Lou:** We were out there for like a week. You did the Notting Hill Carnival didn't you? **Lou:** Yeah, that was love. **Tah:** Yeah, the women out there was nice too. The peoples is prejudiced, I mean they ain't preju-diced, we just didn't understand them. **Spigg:** They got their own slang. **Tah:** I mean out there the language is what it is, it ain't like it out here where there is so many different languages. I mean out

there there's two languages I mean whatever y'all talk. I mean you've got your slang and then you've got your...**Lou:** Proper **Tah:** It's wild. But out here there is so many different talks… black guy, Puerto Rican… our whole conversation is a mixture everything that we would be around. That's why we understand ourselves sometime…We catch ourselves talking more sense than we making 'cos we're on a different point of view. It's real, we get to see a whole different perspective outta life. **Spigg:** What about the new album this is gonna be something for us…That's out next week that's out on Monday in London. Is it here as well? **Spigg:** Nah, that comes out Tuesday (Toosday). On a Tuesday (chooseday)? **Lou:** Chooseday! **Tah:** That's chooseday. CHOOSEDAY!…Ha ha ha!…What else have you picked up from what I was saying, Tuesday and what else? **All:** THINGS! **Tah:** We love y'all, we came back here talking just like y'all, but in our own way. **Lou:** *(Starts shouting in an American / Cockney accent)* HONEY BABY!

HONEY BABY!

EPMD / *Colour Photograph* / SARAH EDWARDS / *Interview* / SALLY EDWARDS   page 104 / 105

THE INNOVATORS,
COMMENTATORS,
PIONEERS,
SLOGANEERS,
THE PROFESSIONALS
WITH THE
CONFESSIONALS…

Blag is in no doubt, honored to meet…'…the ten year veterans, one thousand rap sessions…' **Please introduce yourselves:** *(I turn to Erick…)* **Can you describe Parrish** *(and to Parrish….)* **Can you describe E…***(Oh, he's fallen asleep.)* **Erick:** Get outta here, ha ha, I'd describe us as being EPMD! I'm Erick Sermon, he's Parrish Smith. *Everyone, falls about in fits of laughter.* **Erick:** Erick Sermon, funk lord, always on the board, nice with the mic. Illest b-boy-matic. Nobody can f*** with us. Ha ha ah…How's about Parrish Smith, Mr. Smith, gets with the smittiest, attitude shittiest, f***ed up… *(Parrish Wakes up looks up, pissed off…)* **Erick:** Ay! What's wrong with that?! **Parrish:** I'm mad! **Erick:** Yeah, yeah…**Parrish:** You tell her my attitude is f***ed up…**Erick:** Yeah, yeah yeah. **Parrish:** real shitty…**Erick:** So! *Everyone, falls about in fits of laughter.* **Erick:** Go ahead…

EPMD: THE ENTERTAINERS…

Alright, I'm not going to do a normal interview, this one is split up into different categories… **Parrish:** I'm gonna give you a corny interview now! What! You're give us a corny interview? Damn. **Erick:** Nah never! We'll give you a good interview. **OK, say next time we go to New York, where would you take us out to eat?** **Parrish:** My crib, I'll cook. What do you want? Are you vegetarian? Eat a bit of seafood? **Parrish:** Alright, we'll do some string beans, we'll do whatever you want! You bring the groceries! Ha ha ha. **What about you (Erick) where's the best place to eat?** **Erick:** In New York? Oh man! McDonalds, man! Ha ha ha. Oh, I don't know, we're not really restaurant guys! **Parrish:** We're keepin' it real. **Erick:** Yeah. **Parrish:** We don't be in four star restaurants! We'd be in a Soul Food restaurant eatin' chiplins! You know what chiplins are? **No! Parrish:** Pig intestine, ha ha ha! **Erick:** Make your house smell nice and good! **Mmmm, yeah I bet.** **Erick:** We usually have 'em for thanks giving. **Make up a cocktail with ingredients and name…Do you drink alcohol?** **Erick:** Yeah, I'm a casual drinker, but I drink…Rum and Coke, that's a Fuzzy Navel. **Parrish:** Um, Vodka… sometimes I'll drink some Vodka. A shot of tequila. **Erick:** A bottle of Hennessy… straight. So, would you just sort of line 'em up and drink 'em straight, instead of mixing them together, ha ha ha! **Parrish:** Whatever works at the time! **Tell us five things to get a party started!** **Parrish:** What to get it started! Roll a blunt, get f***ed up! **Erick:** Chill, let the party come to you. *Everyone, falls about in fits of laughter.* **Parrish:** Loud Music, can't hear yourself talk and shit, just cool out. See a girl, just cool out, don't give her too much props. And she'll bug out! **Erick:** To have a good party, the party could be boring. But, you as an individual drinking, or havin' like a little bit of something, just to stimulate…it ain't gotta be much, it can just be one little drink. And you can start up your own situation, and everything will be alright.

EPMD THE INNOVATORS

Do you know what blag means? Both: no. **OK, say if I was to try and get some of your drink there, it's basically you have to be a bit cheeky and it's to get something without for it! You know, like getting into a club without paying! So, how would you blag your way into a blag party?** **Erick:** As bein' me?! Oh yeah! I'm Erick Sermon! Ha ha, you can't say that! **Erick:** Oh, OK! Let me think of somethin'! **Parrish:** I'd go outside and start dissin' the party, when people come in! Oh, huh thanks! **Erick:** I'd be like, I'm a talent scout for Dr. DRE. **Parrish:** We heard all about your magazine and…**Erick:** Here's my card! Take it! **If you're gonna star in a film, say it's a film that's already been made and you're gonna take over the main role, what film would it be and what part would you play?** **Parrish:** Free Willy *Everyone, falls*

about in fits of laughter. **Parrish:** I'd play the little kid! **Erick:** If I was to take over the lead role…pauses… I can't do this shit! Jerry Maguire!! **Tell us the best things to do when it's hot!** **Erick:** Swim, go in a jacuzzi…smoke weed…**Parrish:** turn on the AC. **Erick:** Drink a 40, video.

EPMD THE COMMENTATORS…

Say you had a pirate radio station. Can you do a jingle each? Also, you have to make up the name of the station. **Erick:** Good Evening, this is W.E.P.M.D, today's weather is 109° out this moth-erf***er…**Parrish:** And if you haven't got A.C - yo' ass is f***ed up! **Erick:** And we back with that new shit coming up from EPMD, yes, we play all our shit! *Everyone just falls about in fits of laughter.* **Erick:**…back in a minute…

THE SLOGANEERS…

Tell us some EPMD lingo…Parrish: Audi 5000, the bosack, Macdosious…**Erick:** All that stuff that you hear people use, that's our shit! **Parrish:** Blazin' **Erick:** We had that in '82. **Parrish:** Yeah, nobody didn't know what that was! **Erick:** We had that in '82, when we was in 10th grade.

THE COMEDIANS…

Right, I've pretty much run out of questions. I know, I know this sounds corny, but can you tell us a joke? **Bernard:** *(EPMD's manager, who has been sitting in the corner the whole time pipes up…)* I got one! A quick one! Minnie Mouse and Mickey Mouse are at the Courthouse, they're trying to get a divorce. The judge say's 'Mickey, I can't grant this.' He say's I want to speak to you in one of my chambers! Cracking up…Minnie goes back in the chambers and comes back a half an hour later! **Erick:** Minnie or Mickey? **B:** Minnie, she's comes out of the Judges chambers about half an hour later, and the Judge say's 'You know, I can't understand why you really want to get divorced. And Mickies like, 'Nah! Minnies f***ing Goofy! *Everyone, falls about in fits of laughter.* **Erick:** Stephen Speilberg was shooting this movie…blazin' blazin' movie. He had like a 10 million dollar set. And there's one scene, you know fires' supposed to happen, horses going flyin', smoke, explosions the whole nine! So, he's like 'F*** it, I ain't gonna miss this scene, I'm gonna get three cameras on this! So, yeah, one camera that way, one camera that way and one camera that way!' And he says, 'There's no way, I'm missin' this scene! So, all of a sudden, they get ready to shoot…ACTION , boom horses flyin', f***in' explosions, fire, people runnin', the whole nine! Shit's goin' off, and he's like, 'Cut!' Everyone's like *(clapping his hands)* 'Yeah, yeah, way to go!' So, Stephen's like 'Camera one, did you get that shot? *(everyone in hysterics)* ''Er, nah nah there's something wrong with my camera, my camera didn't work.' Stephen's like, 'Oh don't worry about it, Camera two, you got that shot?' He's like 'Yeah, I got a little bit, but after a while the fire hit the lens…' and he goes 'Alright, Camera three did you get that shot?' and he goes 'Ready when you are Stephen!' *Everyone falls about in fits of laughter.* **Erick:** Ha ha ha, ah….oh dear!!!

THE TEN YEAR VETERANS, ONE THOUSAND RAP SESSIONS

Alright! That's about it, can you make an i-d for blag? **Erick:** Yo, wassup! This is Erick Sermon. **Parrish:** This is Parrish Smith…**Erick:** EPMD, back in business, you know what I'm sayin' **Parrish:** You know what I mean and we're cooling with blag, hip hop with the slang drag… **Erick:**…when you wanna read somethin', read blag…**Parrish:**…word up…**Erick:**…recognise that shit…phattest hip hop, phattest hip hop magazine. **Parrish:** Yeah, Peace.

Contains excerpts from 'Never Seen Before' by EPMD.

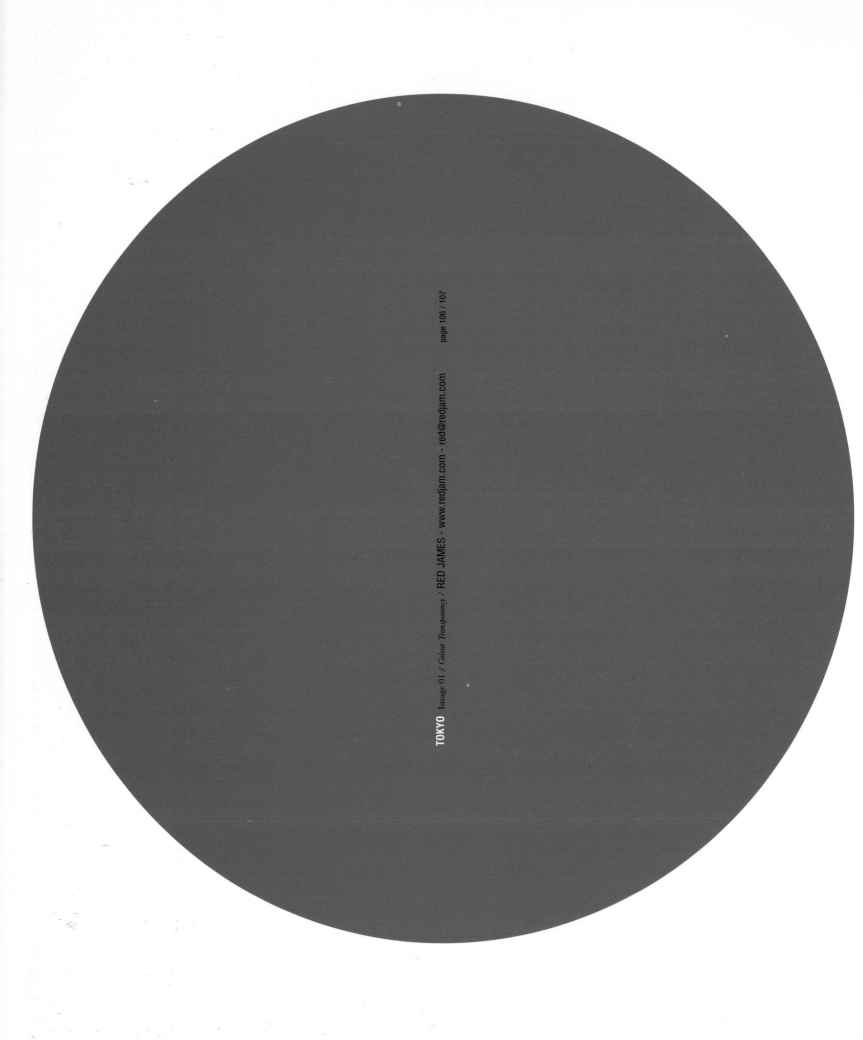

TOKYO Image 01 / *Colour Transparency* / RED JAMES - www.redjam.com - red@redjam.com　　page 106 / 107

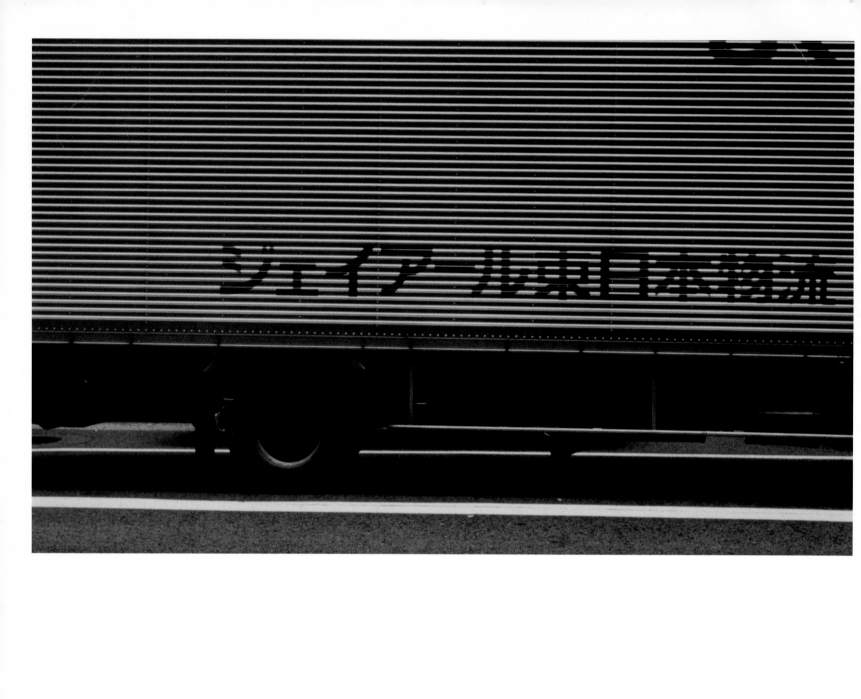

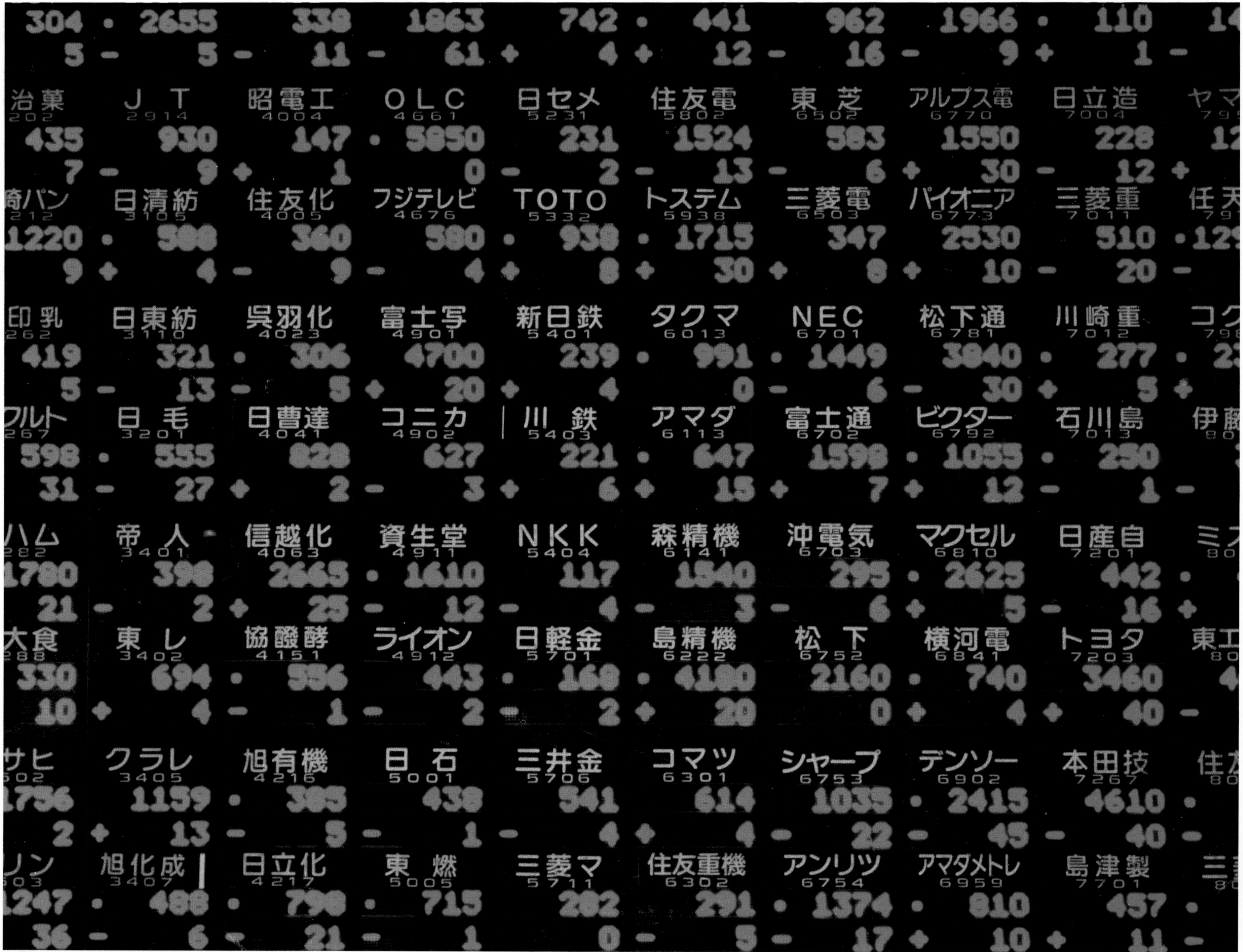

304 · 2655 338 1863 742 · 441 962 1966 · 110
5 - 5 - 11 - 61 + 4 + 12 - 16 - 9 + 1 -
J T 2914 昭電工 4004 OLC 4661 日セメ 5231 住友電 5802 東 芝 6502 アルプス電 6770 日立造 7004
435 930 147 · 5850 231 1524 583 1550 228
7 - 9 + 1 0 - 2 - 13 - 6 + 30 - 12 +
日清紡 3105 住友化 4005 フジテレビ 4676 TOTO 5332 トステム 5938 三菱電 6503 パイオニア 6773 三菱重 7011
1220 · 588 360 580 · 938 · 1715 347 2530 510
9 + 4 - 9 - 4 + 8 + 30 + 8 + 10 - 20 -
印乳 日東紡 3110 呉羽化 4023 富士写 4901 新日鉄 5401 タクマ 6013 NEC 6701 松下通 6781 川崎重 7012
419 321 · 306 4700 239 · 991 · 1449 3840 · 277
5 - 13 - 5 + 20 + 4 0 - 6 - 30 + 5 +
日 毛 3201 日曹達 4041 コニカ 4902 川 鉄 5403 アマダ 6113 富士通 6702 ビクター 6792 石川島 7013
598 · 555 828 627 221 · 647 1598 · 1055 · 250
31 - 27 + 2 - 3 + 6 + 15 + 7 + 12 - 1 -
帝 人 3401 信越化 4063 資生堂 4911 NKK 5404 森精機 6141 沖電気 6703 マクセル 6810 日産自 7201
1780 398 2665 · 1610 117 1540 295 · 2625 442
21 - 2 + 25 - 12 - 4 - 3 - 6 + 5 - 16 +
東 レ 3402 協醱酵 4151 ライオン 4912 日軽金 5701 島精機 6222 松 下 6752 横河電 6841 トヨタ 7203
330 694 · 556 443 · 168 · 4180 2160 · 740 3460
10 + 4 - 1 - 2 - 2 + 20 0 + 4 + 40 -
クラレ 3405 旭有機 4216 日 石 5001 三井金 5706 コマツ 6301 シャープ 6753 デンソー 6902 本田技 7267
1756 1159 · 385 438 541 614 1035 · 2415 4610 ·
2 + 13 - 5 - 1 - 4 + 4 - 22 - 45 - 40 -
旭化成 3407 日立化 4217 東 燃 5005 三菱マ 5711 住友重機 6302 アンリツ 6754 アマダメトレ 6959 島津製 7701
1247 · 488 · 798 · 715 282 291 · 1374 · 810 457 ·
36 - 6 - 21 - 1 0 - 5 - 17 + 10 + 11 -

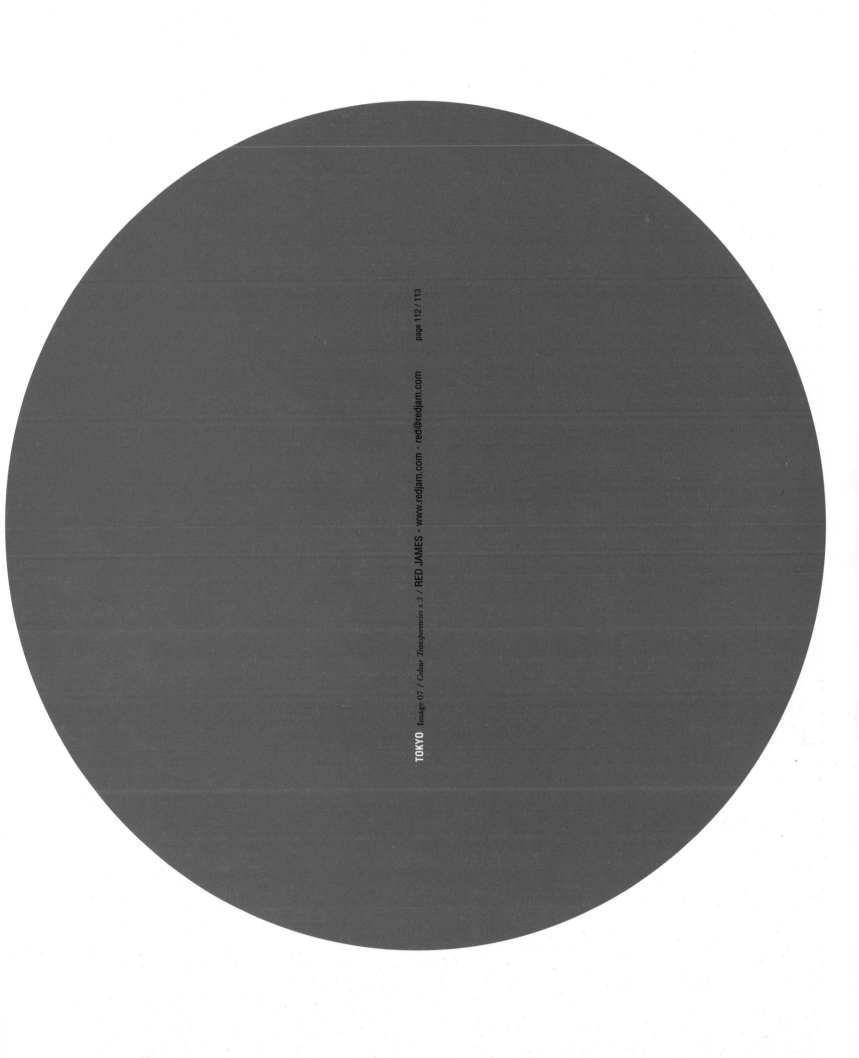

TOKYO Image 07 / *Colour Transparencies x 3* / RED JAMES - www.redjam.com - red@redjam.com   page 112 / 113

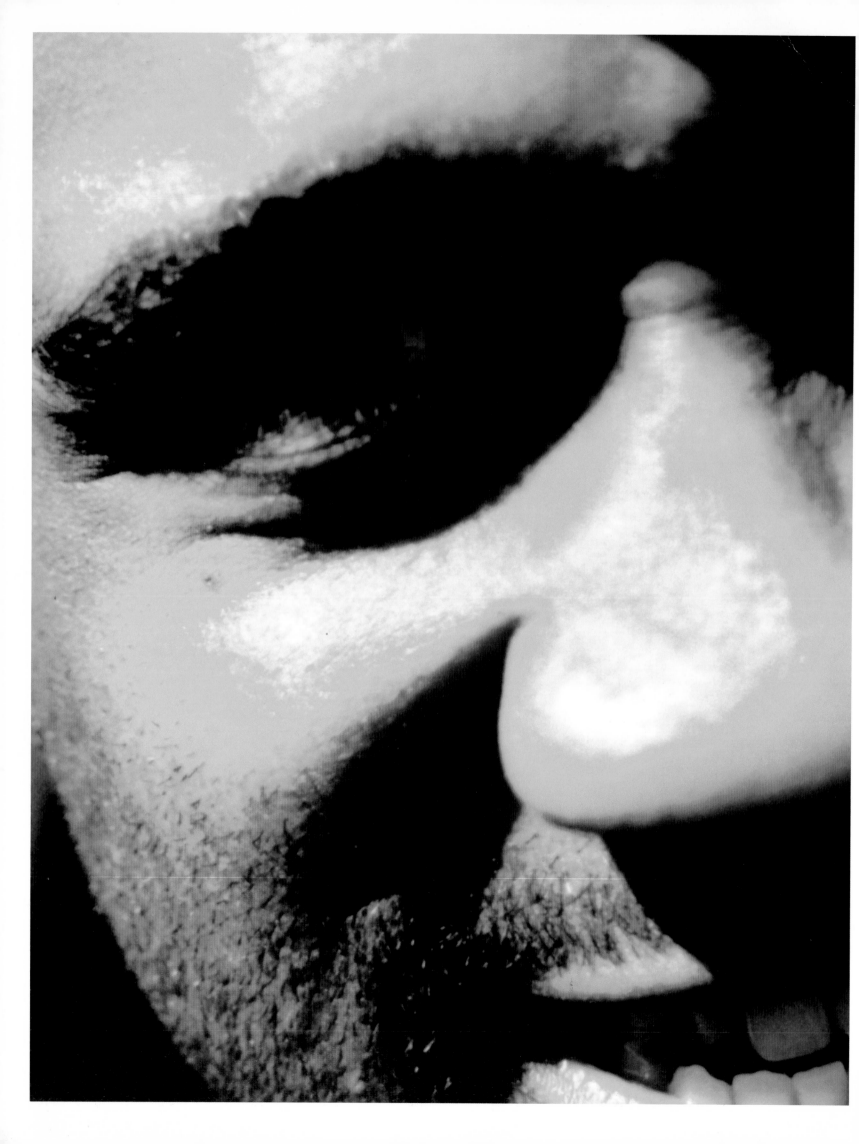

JUNGLE BROTHERS

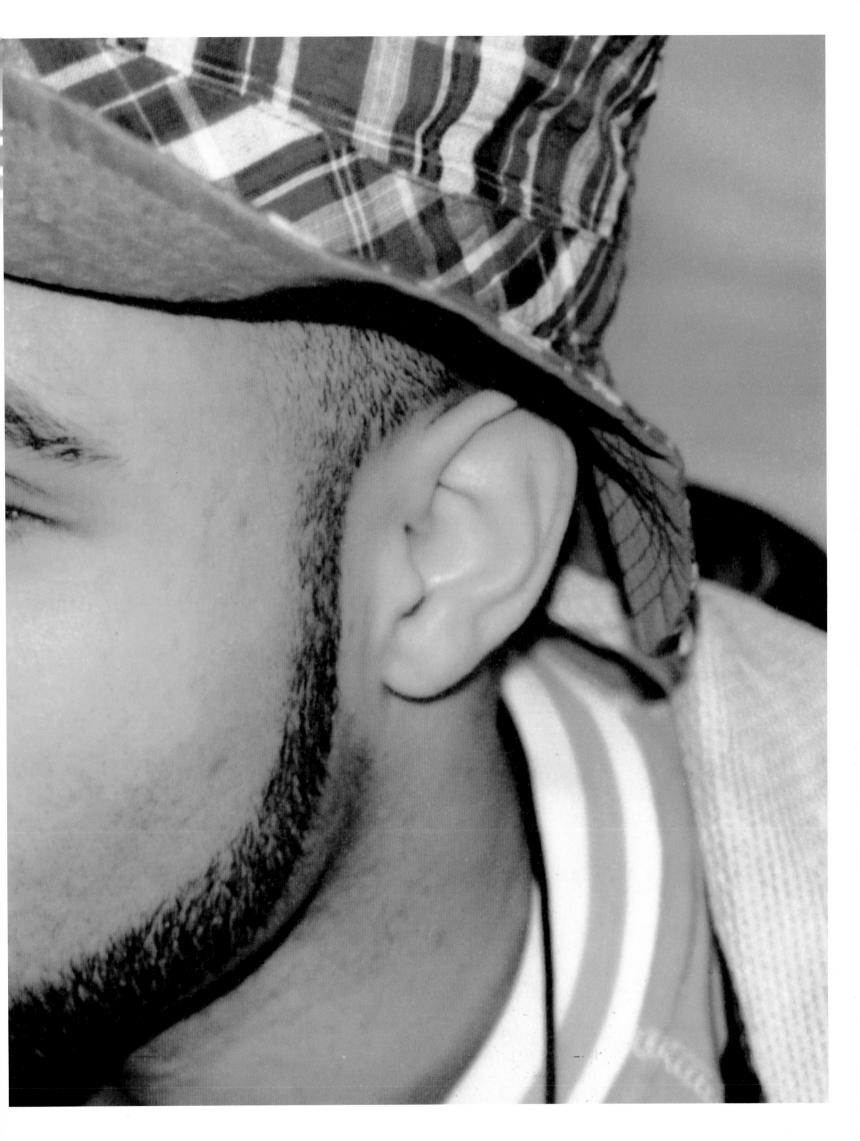

I remember back in my school days, when I was first getting into Hip Hop, I loved this group. I had their name ,amongst others, scribbled on my files and note books. Most of the kids thought I was some kind of nutter, because I wasn't into Bananarama - funny that. I remember dancing and singing round my room to this stuff. This stuff was different; they weren't afraid to experiment with styles. Ten years later they're still not afraid of a bit of diversity. So who am I talking about? Well, it could only be the Jungle Brothers of course. Today I meet Mike G and Afrika to find out what they're all about...

Okay, describe the JBeez including style and sense of humour. **Mike G:** Ai-ight. Well you got myself, Mike G. My style is laid back; I goof at times but the majority is laid back. Then you got Afrika, his style is the same: we goof every now and then, but like, we really stick to topics and get serious at points. What were you like when you were younger ? **Mike G:** Yeah, when we was younger, I mean like 21 or 20, we was into the game. I believe we were doing our second album, 'Done By The Forces Of Nature', and...I almost can't even remember what we was like! Ha ha! Nah, but I was very influenced by the world, because at that time we started doing London a lot, doing a lot of European dates, as well as start touring in The States. So we were really eager to get around, do everything, wanna do everything and touch everything! He he he! You know just like a little kid! Is there any British music that has caught your attention of late? **Mike G:** I like some of the Jungle stuff I hear. I like it when they speed it up, and they be kicking it over, it sounds fat. It's almost like when Hip Hoppers used to experiment back in the days in

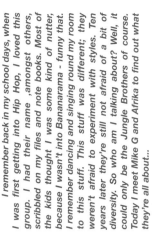

Like if had PlayStation right, they would have something like ClayStation! You know something real stupid, you know and you'd sit there, and you'd make different things with clay. It's real silly. Plus I'd probably put Benny Hill on. What else? A & E, a wildlife show ! Definitely some ESPN. And the fifth one? A music show, Rap City. **Afrika:** In other words my favourite shows? Okay, X Files. I don't watch much television...X Files, ER, The Professionals, The Nutty Professor and New York Undercover. Phew ! Ha ha ! Say you've been asked to stand in for David Letterman? What's happening in in the show? **Mike G:** Oh, I'd have a ball ! I'd have The Roots as the band. You know the band that sits in the corner? That would be The Roots there. Let me see, my first guest...Who would be my first guest? I'd probably have Afrika Bambaataa come on, and then I'd have Dave Mooney. You know Mooney, the comedian? He's an ill comedian. Who else? There's so many people out there: who could I choose? I'd probably have De La Soul, Jungle Brothers, I mean Jungle Brothers?! HA HA HA!! Alright, I'm on now! Ha ha! A Tribe Called Quest ! I'd have a ball, I'd definitely have The Roots rocking before the commercials and also interludes, while we're doing interviews and stuff like that, and I'd show movie clips and all that good stuff. **Afrika:** All Native Tongues are getting interviewed, all Native Tongues are performing: that's my music guests. I'd also have somebody from film to come on. Who would I have from television on my show to get interviewed? Oh, I'd interview Malik Jobah from New York Undercover. The Roots would be the band. I would do a skit, a funny skit of me leaving from behind the desk, of me going to...Damn ! I can't even think of anything !...Oh, I would do a clip of the day in the life of my family, like a family reunion. And I'd have a comedian on there too:

New York, and then to hear this when you come back, it's like "Damn! They almost perfected that". It sounds good as well, as I like the uptempo beats. **Afrika:** I like the hip hop DJs here: The Enforcers, Cutmaster Swift, Pogo and Biznizz. Are there any similarities between London and New York? **Mike G:** Actually not now. From back in the day when we used to come over here, or even a couple of years ago, it seemed liked London was a little behind, but now they know more about the music and everything. The style is definitely more relatable, and nah, there's not too many differences. I guess one thing is, you see more blacks and whites in harmony in London than you see in New York. Besides that, it's almost the same really. Oh, and you have more clubs over here including raves and stuff like that, even certain Hip Hop spots that I've seen. **Afrika:** Any differences and similarities between London and New York? Differences? There is more of a Hip Hop or Rap scene in New York, than there is in London. They're starting to build up more in London though because the DJs and the artists are seeing that they have to make things happen independently themselves, in order for there to be a sustained culture here instead of it just being who-ever is hot for the time being, you know you need more Hip Hop culture here. As well in the States you need more Hip Hop culture too, but that was the birth place you could still find traces of it. If you had a guest spot on a TV station, say 5 shows, what would you have on? **Mike G:** Oh, let me see. I would have Mad TV...You'll have to explain that, we don't know that, sorry. **Mike G:** You don't know Mad TV? Oh it's like real slapstick comedy, like real goofy, making fun of everything.

Eddie Murphy. If not Eddie Murphy, I would have Chris Tucker from Friday. Alright, you've got a guest spot on ER, you can either be the patient, or the doctor: now explain your part. **Mike G:** Oh, I'd definitely be a doctor. I'd be the doctor that splits you open before the operation! Nah, I'd be a brain surgeon. I don't know the characters, but I'd be the brain surgeon who did rap music on the side, so after I've experimented on somebody I'd go do rap shows. Then I'd come back, and the ill scene would be: I come into work one day and I have my DJ on the table, I'd be like 'OH NO !!! OH MY GOD !!' And while I'm here I'll implement a couple of veins! Ha ha ha! **Afrika:** I'd be a doctor...And what would happen? **Afrika:** Okay, I'd be a doctor delivering my wife's baby. I want you to do an advert for TV. How about Turtle Wax for a car? **Mike G:** Mmmm.... Turtle Wax? Ha ha ha! How about Foot Powder? For Athletes Foot?! **Mike G:** Yeah, for Athletes Foot! Ha ha! This is my job: "Hello everybody out there, this is Mike G for 'Foot Funky Foot Powder'. All you bloody non-washing feet fools out there who got foot fungi, use Foot Funky to clean yer feet! Thank you !" After ten years in the business, have you any advice for anyone just starting out there? **Mike G:** Really just learn about the music and know the history, and never be afraid to be innovative, 'cos that's what the music is all about. **Afrika:** Take your time, patience is the most important thing. Any messages? **Mike G:** Just keep your head up, believe in yourself. Even though there's not always space for everybody to be a rapper or DJ, there are many other positions in the business that is needed, especially on the business side.

I'D BE THE BRAIN SURGEON WHO ON THE SIDE DID RAP MUSIC
Mike G

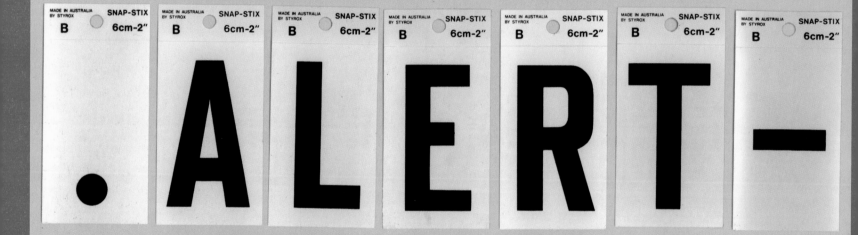

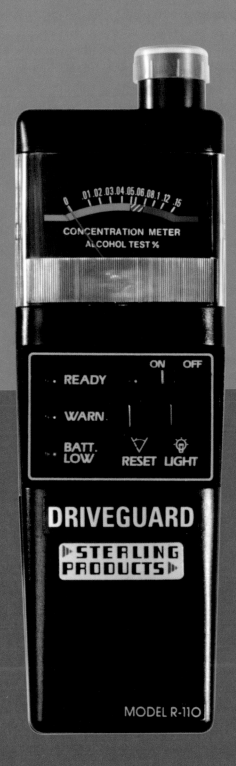

TORNADO

HURRICANE

VIRUS

The Andromeda Strain   Outbreak   The China Syndrome   Virus   Scanners   The Omega Man

MONSTER

Jaws   King Kong   Godzilla   The Land That Time Forgot   Jason & The Argonauts

QUAKE

Earthquake   Last Days Of Pompei   Tremors   The Poseiden Adventure   Rollercoaster

PORNO

Up!   New Wave Hookers   Confessions Of A...   Emanuelle   Debbie Does Dallas

INVASION

ATTACK

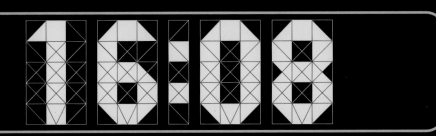

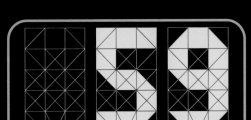 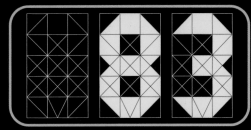

 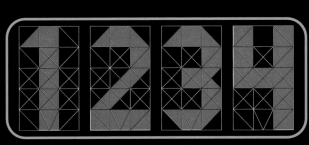 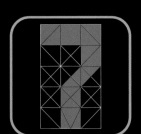

SLUM VILLAGE

BAATIN / *Colour Photograph* / SARAH EDWARDS / *Introductions* / SALLY EDWARDS / *?uestions* / AHMIR ?UESTLOVE THOMPSON

For anyone who knows anything, Slum Village are the most exciting newcomers to the world of hip hop and for me, having an interview booked in with them I definitely want to do something different and exciting. So I'm thinking 'How can I do this one? Shall I do something off key? Like, make it more of a role play?...Use some cards or something?' It's a Saturday in London, and Sarah and I have just been invited to The Roots' sound check in Brixton. We're heading there on the bus and I'm still thinking about how this interview can be different...I know!...How about getting previous blag cover star - Ahmir to do the interview with me? Definitely! He knows all about them. So, we get to the venue and go in. Backstage, we wander the corridors looking for him and head to the stage. "Hey Foxy, have you seen The Roots?" Sarah asks a sound tech friend. "No..." (blah blah blah). So we head back down the corridor.

Then through the glass to the outside of the building I spot his silhouette..."Sarah! There he is! Go get him!" So she runs out. I hear "Sarah!" in an English accent - it's Ahmir - so I follow, and we're greeted with big hugs; then we walk back to the stage, where I pose my question: "Will you interview Slum Village with me on Tuesday? Don't tell them. They think it's just me. I want to surprise them!" "Sure." Cool, so that's that sorted now lets forward to Tuesday...It's about 11:40am and it's chucking it down as I arrive at Ahmir's hotel. "Hi!", I greet the concierge, "Can you let Ahmir Thompson know Sally Edwards is in reception please?" She calls up and next thing I'm in the lift heading to his room. Ring the bell...no answer. Knock really loud...Door opens. "Hey! I was stalling you! Come in." Alright then. So while he finishes his internet work, I wait. "Goodbye" says Mr.AOL. We get set, leave and cab it to the hotel. "It looks like a shed...", says Ahmir. I pay up, we get out and meet the Slum Village lot in the foyer. Sarah arrives shortly after, she's taking the pics today. Loads of greeting and "Heys!" take place. Timothy, SV's manager, says "Did Ahmir bring you?" "No, I brought Ahmir!"..."Oh, no doubt!" he laughs...

Ahmir, Sarah, Jay Dee, T3, Baatin and myself then jump in the lift and head to the suite on floor six...In here we take our seats, T3 heads for the sofa closley followed by Baatin who sits to his left. I sit opposite on a sort of arm chair, Sarah to my right, Ahmir to my left, on another sofa and Jay Dee to his left. How's that for picture setting?! Now, I get the tape recorder and set it up in the middle and give Ahmir - who will be taking up chief interviewer role - the nod. Take it away... Ahmir: Alright, do we really need to go through all the formalities of how you started the group?... Actually I kind of want to know how y'all started the group, because I don't know...Jay Dee, y'all met in high school right? **Jay Dee:** Alright, basically I heard about T3 and Baatin in high school, and they were supposed to be the illest MCs... actually I was the illest MC!! You know, I came to this school, I met them through my brother and we went to T3's crib that day, we'd all just hooked up, because my brother was cool with him so...A: What year was this? **JD:** It was '89. A: You guys were in '89? **JD:** No, like '92. In like '89 we hooked up at T3's crib, freestyling. A: So, that's when Slum Village was born. So, now I'm gonna start cliche-ing myself. Why Slum Village? **T3 giggles:** Hot shit today!!...*Ha ha ha!* A: No, these are the only three cliched joints I'm asking and that's it for today! **T3:** How did we get the name? We were just looking up in the dictionary all types of stuff, trying to think of something witty that could describe the sound, because we was doing all kinds of gritty beats back then, but now we've got a whole new definition of what Slum Village is, it's like a contradiction of things, Slum you think of city, Village you think of hills and all that. It's sort of like out music on how we like to blend different shit together, you know soft music with hard lyrics.

"JAY DEE COMES WITH THE PLAN..."

A: The thing that struck me about y'all when I first got 'Volume I' was that you could clearly see three distinct personalities, something that you rarely see in hip hop groups, usually one member outshines the other two, or you can't make a distinction, but in here you know you got a mad scientist of sonic structure. **Ahmir points at Jay Dee, then looks to T3...**You got...a somewhat...How would I describe you T3?! Because you're nasty with your shit!! **T3:** Oh! Am I really nasty?! A: And Baatin to me is just a maniac on stage! He's the superstar. As far as decisions are made, is this a democracy situation? Like how are decisions made in the group, because I come from a six man group in which... I see this as a democracy, but at the end of the day it's me and Tariq that decide what goes on, just at the end of the day, you know what I'm saying. **T3:** Most of the times Jay Dee comes with the plan, I may have a little input and then Baatin he really be at the last minute on the input. So, it's usually Jay Dee, then me, then Baatin, and it's like 'Well, I'm ready to roll whatever's going on' - that's usually Baatin's motto.

"BRINGING FOCUS BACK TO DETROIT..."

A: So, speaking of which, and I know you'll get asked this a million times seeing as you're from the same city. I'm noticing right now that Detroit is on an up surgence with... at least as far as Kid Rock and Eminem are concerned, bringing focus back to Detroit. Which most people that I rap to now, their impression of Detroit is like the poor white trash hip hop capital, you know there's these two artist that have rewritten the history of black music! *At this point we're interupted by the television turning itself on, which evokes our attention.* **JD:** Wooh...Mystery TV!...*Everyone laughs*...Back to A: I mean what do you think... you guys are gonna take the long road to prestige as far as coming out of Detroit. I mean you guys to me are the epitome of what classic East Coast hip hop should be sounding like, and not a place where hip hop on the East Coast doesn't even sound like it's from the East Coast anymore. You guys sort of just pulled a coo on taking up the time back to Detroit. Is there any pressure to?...because I've been around your spot, and y'all and the flock y'all roll with are the only group of people that I know are in that mentality of progressiveness. You know, is there any temptation whatsoever to go to Master P's side of the woods? Or how do you dance on that fine balance of making progressive music, and still trying to rap to Detroit at the same time and getting the Detroit lot to feel y'all like we feel y'all? ***T3 explains this situation:*** Maybe at the beginning it was more depression when we didn't have the deal, more so than now because we was on the verge, like let's say when we made 'Get Dis Money', originally we made 'Get Dis Money' so we could get radio play just in Detroit. It's an old song that we were just gonna put out on CD so Detroit can feel us, but we kept it and all that as you know. So we was trying to adapt, but still keep our own stuff, like okay say we can do this and we can do this over here as well, so what we try to do is, incorporate that in the music without going into somebody else's stuff. You know what I'm sayin'? Okay, so if Slum Village do a song about making money and dancin' and all that, it's still not going to be what you have heard before you see, you know what I'm saying? Okay, so if we gonna take it there, we gonna take it there our special type of way, so you can kind of feel us, but we ain't selling ourselves like changes what we do anyway as a group, so we try to incorporate that in one big nutshell. You know?

THE REASON WHY BLAG ENLISTED ?UESTLOVE FOR THIS INTERVIEW...

A: So, has we sort of put a pressure on you guys to sort of carry at the time, because when I first heard y'all man, I was...ha ha ha ha!!! Sorry man! I was like Yo man! Like when I hear shit and I feel it, like I'm just a motherf***er that'll make a motherf***er hear some shit at gun point and force 'em, and sometimes, and I'll be honest with you, sometimes I've gone so far across the line of explaining y'all, that I've actually made some motherf***ers hate y'all, because I've been so over-the-top with this shit that when they've got it, they're like 'What the f*** is this?' and it's like... If I see like-minded people doing shit, I'm gonna flock towards them because like, sometimes you feel like you're the only motherf***er out there feeling your shit, and when other people are doing the shit that you enjoy you know what I'm saying like...How do y'all deal with that pressure? You know, because I've calmed down on the temptation of making motherf***ers listen and buy your shit, haha! I'm sorry man! I know y'all meet this journalist who's like 'You know Ahmir from The Roots, I've got these whip lashes from...' No! Hahaha !! I'm just saying is there an actual pressure to take the Baatin away, or not take the Baatin away...**T3:** What d'you think about that Baatin? **Baatin:** I don't feel like there's pressure, it began to get pressured when heavyweight motherf***ers start coming up and shaking your hand like 'What's up man? Ya'll ill y'all.' And it's like damn man! This is The Roots talking to us, you know what I'm saying? This is D'Angelo telling us we're dope, it feels like damn !... like our next song!'...**T3 laughs**...The motherf***ers we're listening to! You know what I'm saying? **B and JD in stereo:** Our next song's gonna be ridiculous!! **T3:** Well, you know it's good because it gives us this kind of competition thing, okay, I like The Roots, The Roots like me, but we still gotta win! It's always like that - you know how artists are! So it gives us motivation you see and know somebody you actually know for instance, like me and Jay Dee, I've got to come with some type of beat so I can play Jay Dee, so he won't be looking at like, 'Get that off!' you know what I mean! ...**JD laughing**...Turn it off ! **T3 laughs back:** Yeah, you nasty! A: So what were you're initial reactions seeing slow press people not really understand where you're coming from? **T3:** When you're doing something different and people don't understand. It's stuff to say in slots, you either got, 'I'm hip hop', 'I'm this type of guy', 'I'm the rough guy in the street'. They don't have people just playing along all types of lines, and people like to put you in one category, so when they did that I was like, they don't understand where we're coming from, half the articles is wrong and all that...but you know I'm not sweating that, as long as we just get out there and do the best we can A: Yeah that's my advice, because I get caught in that shit, because...Tip, even though he says it doesn't, I know that shit affects him sometimes...**JD:** Hahaha! Just a little bit ! A:...You know I'm arguing with The Source person, like 'Damn, you didn't even say what made the shit good...**Slum Village:** Right, right right. A: ..Like I don't know, just to say that journalism is down, where you just got motherf***ers who don't even know this is a five barred loop, you know what I mean, basic shit, so it's like I don't know, but this is what I do want to know...**JD:** What's that? A: What's up with your overall lifestyle in Detroit and y'all showing the world the rest of Detroit, I mean what is Detroit about? **B:** Detroit, as far the music goes is like three separate communities of choices of music. You got a very small community of motherf***ers who listen to hip hop, you got a large, the largest, the one in the middle of ones who listen to R&B, booty shaking music which is considered techno, house music and commercial R&B hip hop and you got a small percentage who are just getting higher, who listen to rave and the deep techno...A: Cos that shit was invented in Detroit, I mean some people don't even know that. **B:** Exactly, so you got your section who listen to that, that's like the acid heads, you know what I'm saying? So, where we come in, we fit in in all three of them, I'm the one as far as us individually, I'm the one who's politic in all three of them areas, I go to all the venues in Detroit, I know where everything's at, you know what I'm saying? As far as Jay Dee, he knows where all the entertainment venues is, that's where he politic at. You know that. A: In Philly motherf***ers be playing their own music in your car in three seconds, like you know what I mean? Like they know their video is about to come on and whatever, and they'll have it on, they'll have the joint on in the room looking right at it!...Y'all is just so cool with your shit, and I'm like, how can y'all be so disciplined as far as and especially when I'm up in Detroit? How can y'all be so cool about you're shit like this ain't the second coming? **T3:** Like number one is we've seen a lot of people, I had some friends that was in a group and they was doing their thing, and they

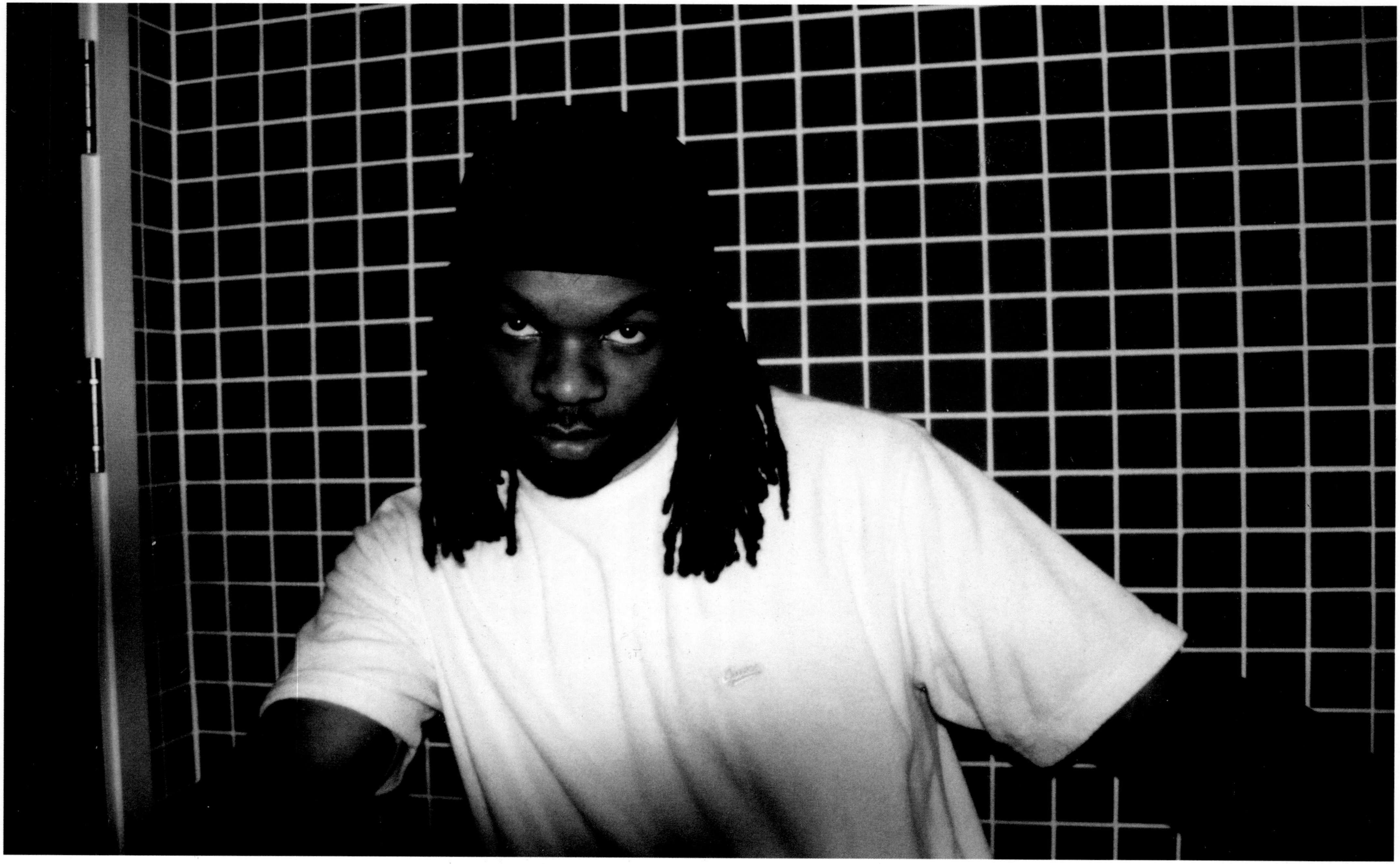

was getting a little bigger than us in the D, you know what I'm saying? We was on the same type of stuff, but they got big and then there egos got big, and we always said we weren't going to be this type of guy. Like you know, and we're not gonna get sweet regardless of what ever we do haha ! We said we're not going to get sweet, and he got sweet you know and all he's got is a CD on the rack and that inspired us to make 'Fantastic Volume 1' and we're like 'Okay, y'all think you're doing it now, give us a week!' *Haha !!* **B gets out of his seat:** Okay dude. This is backstage footage, we came to the show with backpacks like the old school days, with 200 tapes, no that night we only brought 150…Dude, soon as we walked in the club all we did was pull out one tape and sssssssspppppppp!! *(Impersonates getting run at and surrounded by.)* It was bananas man ! Once the taste was out there it was over, forget about it.

"OH STOP PLAYIN'!!! HAHAHA!!!"

Oh stop playin'!!! Hahaha!! **A:** You've also got to be the most bootlegged…well you're signed now but, y'all are the most bootlegged, at least 'Fantastic Volume I' is the most bootlegged I've seen. **B:** "You think so? The first one? **A:** Yo man, proof, I've been around the world. Like I went to Portland, some cat was trying to sell me that shit for $50, Virginia wanted $30 for the shit, I got the ?uestlove discount haha! You go on line now, your albums downloaded on at least 20 programmes. I mean shit don't get dangerous, to me that just adds to your legend you know, and I'm not really looking for record sales to be my choice of income, but how did y'all personally act when people were coming to you telling you that your shit is everywhere, like that didn't even happen to us, you know what I'm saying? Like that buzz is such an important factor in launching a group, you know and I know a least 10,000 hits, you know 'Fantastic' is on at least three bootleg labels alone, so did you really expect it to just do that like it did, like hot cakes? **T3:** Of course not like that, you know we knew we put a lot into that album and especially the 'Volume 1' we know we put a lot into that. **A:** How long did it take y'all to do that by the way? **JD:** We made that in four days. They came to me and was like 'Yo, we need to put a tape out, and I'm like cool shit. I gotta leave outta town Saturday, and it's like Monday and I came up with all them beats and… **A:** Oh stop playin'!!! Hahaha!! **JD:** Yo, we was over there rhyming to click tracks and high hats and they leave, and I come back like fired on fire and I gotta remix this joint. Like ts-ts-ts-ts. **A:** So y'all do the music last? Before…**Another SV chorus:** Mostly. **A:** Don't say that man! **B:** Okay, let me tell you. We did 'Estimate' like that, like 'ts-ts-ts-ts-ke-ts-ts-ts-ts-ke' and all our solo versions and all of those skits we did it like that…**A:** "WHAT!!!??? HAHAH AHAHAHOHOHOHO !!!!!!!…JD continues the story:** I'm like 'Baatin, you've got to lay down a verse'…**B:** And I'm like 'You got a high hat? I'll do it a cappella…' **JD:** And I'm like 'I got a high hat and a snare man.' **A:** Oh please don't loose that shit, I don't care what happens. I got people who've got to have the final mix now before they can write a verse, I'm telling you! There should be no reason why there is like 90 two inch reals, there should be like 20 songs not like 160 because she got to hear the final mix, strings included, flying people in to do background just to see if she's going to rhyme to that shit. That just leads into my next shit, like y'all style the patented adverb background chanting, I don't know how I would articulate this on paper, it's like a syncopated-harmonic background vocal where they just rock a bunch of adverbs and exclamations in a rhythmic way, sort of like jazz musicians like with 8th notes and 16th notes, and now y'all telling me that y'all weren't even bouncing off the music when y'all did this shit?! **JD:** Right, right… **A:** Y'all just had a click track for a whole bunch of those…So, when you were doing your lyrics you had a prototype of a whole different song in your mind, that you hadn't even constructed yet… **JD:** Right, right. **A:** Damn, I feel this small man. **J:** Like sometimes we'll come up with a little sub quest or something. Like I'll try and make a bass line to that, you know what I'm saying… **A:** So that explains why, 'cos I was about

to say, when you do your pattern and accent shits on certain syllables, you know I thought it was the sort of thing where you were sitting there counting forever, but it was done first so you could just programme…oh! **JD smiles:** Yeah, word. **A:** That's the best shit I heard in my life, damn! So, y'all made that shit in four days? **T3:** We was real hungry man !

"OOOOHHHHHHHHH!!!"

A: So who was the group that just licked your ass? **JD:** I ain't telling you the group ! **A:** It's cool, it's blag ! **Here comes another one of those Slum Village chorus:** Arrghhh! Ha ha ha ha!!! **A:** It's blag, this ain't Right On, this ain't Black Beat, tell the truth! Do they know that they brought this record to life? **JD calms down:** Yes they do, because 'Players' was about them, and another song's about them and actually they were on that song. **A:** HAHAHAHA !!!! **B takes up the story:** And what was funny…they're on the album! **A:** Oh, just to prove that you had no beef with them? **JD:** Well, I wouldn't say beef, we had a little rivalry with them… **A:** Oh, yeah everyone has a little rivalry… **JD:** Okay, that was like the last thing, I did a little beat and…**B butts in:** And to make it funny we put 'Players' on right after their song, just on purpose! Hahaha! **A:** Wait a minute, where are they right now? **T3:** Well Proof is with Dirty Dozen, they be doing some stuff. **JD:** Loud has Proof. **A:** Didn't I see him with Eminem? **T3:** Hhmmm yeah, he's Eminem's sideman, and the other two are living in New York. **A:** So, did they have a bangin' twelve inch that you just felt and you just…? **JD:** No, no they was doing a lot of shows, they had a crew, was it Boom Squad? **A:** Yeah. **JD:** Yeah, you know what I'm saying and they was just out there, people started knowing about them. **A:** You see they used to roll with us and they called themselves Hip Hop Gs, it was nasty, they know it was wack… **B:** But their egos was so large man. They thought they were Gods man, they used to come in the place man, with their matching jackets. **T3:** They used to come into the place with shirts and ties on man ! *B gets out of seat again…*I come in the place right, St.Andrews. Walk in, there's one over there…this is my family man ! I used to stand in circles with this cat, playing you know? I'm like 'What's up man?' *(mimes hand shake, hug etc)* and he's like 'Wait, wait I got to get in this shot' *(mimes the kid running into a group shot across the way).* The dude didn't come back, I'm like waiting. I'm was soooo…**Everyone:** OOOOOOHHHHHHHH !!! **A:** Yo, man when motherf***ers front on you. That to me; I love it when motherf***ers front on me, because that just makes you want to make some shit, you know what I mean, when you're underestimated, that is just the best possible shit in the world. **T3:** Oh yes, it definitely is. **A:** So, did they ever find out 'Players' was about them? **T3:** Oh yes they did, you see me, Baatin and these three other guys used to have this spiritual circle going on. We used to do spiritual stuff together and it was another guy right. This in between guy right, he used to come over to my house because I used to make beats for him, so I told him 'You know what 'Players' is about?' You know we just kicking it as homeboys. No no no no, see 'Players' was about that group and a guy who used to talk to my girl, and that's a whole 'nother situation, see what happened was me and this guy used to be cool right? Now, him and my girl they dated once or twice and it was cool, so I called him up and was like 'Man don't let this be getting me being hurt.' and he's got women, about five or six and he's like 'If I ain't with her, you ain't either' so you know we're kicking it and I see him in this place after work and we have this talk and he said cool, he still loves her, he's upset, he can't deal with it and then you know he's doing his thing and we're doing it, and it turns into a big beef and we're not even cool today. So, anyway I was talking to this guy and what happened is; he just drifts off, I ain't seen him for about two months. Now he's cooling with them, he's chilling with them now. So now they know everything, and they come to us saying 'How y'all gonna do a song about us like that?' and they bring it to the spiritual circle like that, and I'm saying 'Why you wanna bring that? That's like business, this is like our church' and whatever you want to call it, 'Let's not bring it here', but they just couldn't deal with it. So, that's what happened, we talked about it

WE MADE THAT IN FOUR DAYS. THEY CAME TO ME AND WAS LIKE 'YO WE NEED TO PUT A TAPE OUT, AND I'M LIKE COOL SHIT, I GOTTA LEAVE OUTTA TOWN SATURDAY, AND IT'S LIKE MONDAY AND I CAME UP WITH ALL THEM BEATS

Jay Dee on the making of 'Volume I'

and I was like 'Why don't y'all just do a song about us? Call it a day, we're not upset.' You know what I'm saying?! Ha ha!

BAATIN'S A MANIAC MAN !

A: Damn, I need some X-Rated shit for blag man. **B:** What you on about? **A:** That shit on your record, y'all pimps man, y'all from Detroit. Y'all roll with pimps, I know y'all got some shit man! Hahaha! Alright, what happened on Friday! *T3 starts grinning:* Oh Baatin was a maniac on Friday ! **JD:** Yeah, a maniac ! **T3:** He had one group of girls, then another group of girls. **JD:** Baatin's a maniac man! **T3:** Then he brought two home ! Baatin was a maniac !! **B:** Man, it was that wine she bought me. *Everyone:* Arrrggghh!...Ha ha ha ha ha ha!!... *JD starts creasing up:* You got to see Baatin, man! We gotta send him the tape ! **A:** You're crazy man, some NWA type shit, us man we're just Grandfathers now! As soon as the shows finished we're like, 'Where's the van?'. **JD:** No, no, we're not like that... **A:** Alright, so y'all have been on tour for a little second what's the spot that's feeling y'al? *B fires in:* Philly, oh forget about Philly! *A squeals:* WHAT?!!! **T3 to A:** Philly's crazy man, you was at the show...**A:** I know that, but tell me, tell me, tell me...**T3:** Oh man Philly is nice man, we love Philly. **A:** Oh man, Philly is cheap man. You can buy or rent a crib in the Philly's version of Manhattan, for like 800 bucks - three storeys - six bedrooms - three bathrooms... **B:** WHAT?!! No, no, that's bananas man! **A:** Shit, our apartment in Manhattan was 4000 a month and it was half the size. **A:** Alright, who are y'all feeling right now in hip hop? *SV simultaneously insist:* Lootpack. **T3:** The beats alone is dope, because they've just got some real sloppy, like rugged, but they're dope. **B:** Lootpack remind me of when we was in the basement and shit you know what I'm saying, like old school when we was sweating in the basement.

"OH!! THE MOTHERF***ING SCIENTIST!"

A: So, when y'all first started what was it you were using? **T3:** MPC60 and the SP1200, and the S950. **JD:** I used to dig inside the tape player and turn the pitch down, I used to freak that shit. **B:** Let me tell this story man. You used to go down to his basement man, and see this broken tape deck right, a mixer and the receiver, a big ass stereo...**JD:** My Mum's stereo. **B:** The ones that go 'ooooooooohhhh'. So, the tape deck is broken in half like a coconut or something, and this guy man is like 'Y'all gotta check this beat out man, hold on...' and puts a wire on and that like, it was normal. *Everyone:* Ha ha ha ha! **B:** And then the album, man! How he broke his loops down, this cat'll take a razor blade and cut out certain songs, take a safety pin and scratch out certain loops to loop the shit man, that old - old school eighties thing... **A:** Hahahahaha!!! You ain't right man!! So, you're telling me y'all was rhyming to a click track, for one of my all time favourite records and now y'all telling me while I was home just pressing a pause tape, you was literally taking drum breaks and slicing the shit in the middle thus making the shit loop...**B:** Yeah, he was like 'Yo man, I wanna use this sound man, but this guitar is too damn loud.' Oh!! The motherf***ing scientist! *JD takes up the story:* I figured out how to filter the sound, so you've got the whole shit, but you can take it out and just hear the sample. I had it where I could just get the guitar and shit, or I can record it three or four times, turn the treble all the way down and filter it to the bass line. **A:** You're stupid man! Do you ever do that thing where you take a walkman and you have the headphone Jack halfway out...? **JD:** I did that shit, I did that with the... **A:** You did that shit?! Oh man!! **JD:** Yeah, I'm trying to figure out that shit with the 1200, I gotta figure that shit out. **A:** Oh man! Stop playin'!!! **JD:** Yo, figure that shit with the stereo man! Ha ha! **A:** Oh no! I thought this shit only worked with a walkman! **JD:** I'm trying to get like just JB drums and shit. **A:** So, when did you get your first machine? **JD:** I didn't get my machine 'til like '93 -'94, haha! '94 was when I got the 950. **A:** See I just cheated I would get a breakbeat record that played the loop over and over again,

and SK1 that shit. **JD:** Oh hahaha !!!...

"SHAKE IT UP, SHAKE IT UP, SHAKE IT UP, SHAKE IT UP, SHAKE IT UP..."

A: So, I guess the last thing I want to talk about is just the overall production; which is like bananas. You know there is just musical ideas being conveyed that just aren't music anymore? I'm sure you're now at the point were you're like, 'Okay, the sickest thing I do, will be the best thing I do.' Like, I'm sure right now whenever you make the beat or whenever y'all collaborate on beats, you try and make it as sick as you can make it. You know because motherf***ers like me are just going to jump out a window when we hear this shit, but there has to have been at one point when you've realised that 'Oh shit, I'm gonna start making like sick beats.' Like just making a beat like, just making 'You Gots To Chill' like oh yeah, bang and then there's making a beat, like when did you first realise and calve your niche out, because that's the thing to do. I mean this is the age of Pete Rock and Premiere, it's hard to find what your corner of hip hop production is going to be so that your shit sounds unique, you got motherf****ers out doing your shit. So when was the first time you said 'This is my stamp of approval, this is my shit, this is my patented.'? Like the first time you high resolutioned your drum time... high resolution is when you use human time, like it's not quantized, it's off beat so to speak. **JD:** I can't remember, it was when I first started using high resolution...**A:** Was it The Pharcyde record? **JD:** No, it was before that. I don't know man, my shit be changing, I'm trying to flip my own shit again. **B:** That's what we try to do, we're like 'More time !' **A:** The thing is, y'all flip it I know to satisfy yourselves and whatever, but you've got to understand. Like you're in the fifth grade now, there's some motherf***ers who don't even go to kindergarten right now. I played 'Fantastic' to someone before I came here and that was the greatest thing since sliced bread for them, you know what I mean? They played 'Volume I' in a club in Philly, dude's on the instrumental for like ten minutes. Motherf***ers could not get over the keyboard progression. So, I'm saying do you at least know there is a point where you can go back, and motherf***ers will still not feel as though you're outdated or whatever you know what I mean. In other words Stevie Wonder is always looking for that endless next thing, and sometimes I feel as though if he would just go back to being Stevie...**JD:** Like Prince? **A:** Yeah, y'all know what I'm saying. Do y'all feel afraid that you're going to be so far ahead of the game, like will you know that it's cool to come back and do beats like 'We Be Dem'? **T3:** I think we go in cycles though, like let's take it from the beginning when we first started out, me and Baatin was hardcore, strictly hardcore. You take me before then, I was 2 Live Sex. I had a song called 'Bbbbbrrrr f*** 'em'. Then we had that hip hop stage where we was just chants, back in the Leaders Of The New School days. *B gets up and struts round the room:* "We used to walk round a cappella, all the way round town for miles, like...*Everyone: Ha ha ha ha ha ha!!* **T3:** People would be looking at us like 'What?! **B:** Let me tell you something else we would do...*(Baatin gets up about of his seat once again and walks round behind me)*...We used to take a female out of the crowd right, this was in high school, way back. And we'd pull a female out and 'Arrgh there she go...'and circle around her and be like 'Shake it up, shake it up, shake it up, shake it up, shake it up...' *Everyone: Ha ha ha ha!* **B:** But we won't go too far. **A:** I'm just saying don't change it before, you know don't serve the desert before the soup. **B:** You know what? 'Volume I' was probably the end of our cycle, because we had music before then, before 'Volume I' we was on some other shit, so that was kind of like the end of that cycle...**A:** So, 'Volume II is the beginning of another cycle? **B:** Exactly. Definitely different and exciting - don't you reckon?

Big thanks to Ahmir for his time.

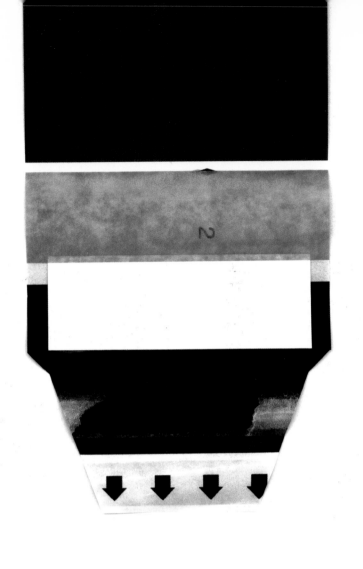

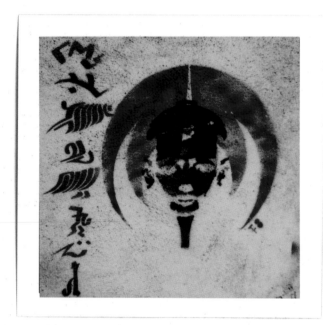

Name: Isabel Marant. **Age:** born in 1967. **Occupation:** Styliste. **Name:** MAI LUCAS. **Age:** 31. **Occupation:** Photographe. **Name:** DJ GILB-R. **Age:** I'm twelve years old. **Occupation:** Several directions involving music, as opposed to one main thing. **How long have you lived in Paris? Isabel Marant:** Always. **Mai Lucas:** I'm born in Paris. **DJ Gilb-r:** That would come to about nine years. **In which neighbourhood do you live? And what do you like about it? I M:** I've lived in two places, in Neuilly, and now the 11th district, between République and Bastille. I chose here because it's what I like in Paris, a blend of people, styles, cultures and age groups. There's a real neighbourhood much like the Paris of old. **Mai Lucas:** I'm now in the 13th, but I've moved around a lot. I was born in the 6th, grew up in Les Halles, then Strasbourg St.Denis, then Stalingrad; finally ending up here between Bercy and the Bibliothèque Nationale. Its 'Les Frigos' (a huge cold-storage building), artists, ateliers. It's a kind of castle rising out of Paris, with everything else knocked down around it. There's lots of space and sky; there's greenery, the Parc de Bercy nearby. We're near the 13th, and Sundays are very lively . You can go do your shopping, and there's loads of Chinese and Indochinese restaurants to go and eat. Across from me there are the 'guinguettes', the barges and riverboats. They're boats on which you can eat and also have a bit of a dance. There's Le Batofar, a floating club, the Péniche Makara that stages African music and concerts. It's not my favourite neighbourhood. I like Paris as a whole but especially around Belleville and rue du Faubourg du Temple. You'll find African hair products, things Indian, and clothes at affordable prices. **DJ G:** I live in the 18th district. At first I lived in the 13th, when I first came to Paris, at La Butte aux Caille; that was pretty cool. I've now been in the 18th for five years or so. What I like about this neighbourhood is it's working class side, that village side, but not in a derogatory sense. I like seeing the children playing in the streets, neighbours talking to each other, going to see my neighbour upstairs if I want to eat something. It's rue de La Goutte d'Or, the 'rootsy' area of the 18th.

Can you recommend any good places to eat, quality wise or cost wise? I M: I adore, 'Chez Janou', not necessarily cheap, but very nice. The spot for good food at small prices is Hoa Li in Belleville, really good Cambodian food. There's Chez Paul in rue de Charonne that's recommended for those visiting Paris; not too pricey, very good food, typically French. Then there's Le Pattaya in rue Étienne Marcel. **Where do you go for socialising? I M:** I love l'Antenne B, boulevard de La Bastille. It's a normal Parisian café on a corner, with sun up till dusk, and the owner is nice. Prices are low, and it's not hip and pretentious. **M L:** Le Café Beaubourg is a pretty good spot for a business-type meeting. The place is nice, not too crowded, and the staff are real polite. **What places do you recommend for parties? I M:** It's better to find a party at someone's house. **M L:** The Globo on Thursday nights is really good. La Java is a good spot if you want salsa on Fridays. I'd avoid places like Les Bains Douches or theme-nights. **DJ G:** I wouldn't advise clubs or cafés, I would go walking in Paris instead, on the river bank, through gardens and parks. I like nature.

Describe Paris season by season, the climate and the activities that go on...I M: Autumn's the time for parties; people are back from their holidays, and the weather's nice until october. There's the fashion shows, parties everywhere, and lots of people from abroad. Winter's a bit of a pain, better go off elsewhere for Christmas and the New Year. Spring means more fashion shows; I like Paris when there's not just Parisians, you meet new people. Summer's the same, with more people and friends coming from all over to visit. **M L:** Parisians are the type of people who show their warmth when the sun's out, so it's not so easy in winter to make new friends if you're from abroad, to find people in that open friendly mood. Luckily there's the cafés, and places to go walking. It's a city full of museums and exhibitions, so there's always major shows on for those visiting; painting, photography, or whatever. There's events on, and you just need to be a bit plugged in on the music or fashion end to find parties going on. In the summertime, the French put on their best profile; there is this Latin side of a certain outgoingness and willingness to conversate. Summer's fun with the swimming pools and its well-tende park lawns; the Parc Montsouris's quite beautiful. I like to go to Les Buttes Chaumont, you could sunbathe, hang out and so on. **DJ G:** I don't like winter, it's a bit sad, paradoxically I don't like the night so much. In winter I wake up pretty late; it's a lethargic period for me. In spring the trees start to sprout and the air changes, leading on to summer which is what I prefer. I like autumn too, I love it's mellow side, I really like the colours of autumn a lot.

Your best or most unusual experience in this city...M L: Back in the days, I remember our hangout being Le Diable de Lombards. That's where we would find out what was going on with the parties. One Saturday or Sunday afternoon in summer, we didn't have anything to do. This friend of ours who we always thought was a bit broke proposed to invite us all around his place. There were about ten of us, and we found ourselves at his place in Neuilly, some huge three-storey house with a swimming pool. So we ended up in the pool with our improvised swimwear, still freaking out about this guy who we'd known for years living in a place like this!

Name: HARDY. Age: Occupation: STYLE GURU (MAHARISHI) Residence: LONDON. **How long have you lived in London?** For 15 years. **Where's the best: a) area?** Inside Holland park Japanese Gardens, Primrose Hill, Hyde Park, Highgate Woods. **b) place to eat?** Breakfast - Organic Cafe, Lonsdale Rd, West London. Lunch - Eastwest Centre, Macrobiotic Restaurant, City Rd. East London. Anywhere that sells good organic food with a nice vibe and also the vegan menu at The Ivy, WC2. **c) place to socialise?** Kashmir Club, downstairs at The Baker & Oven, Paddington St. **d) place to party?** In my front room or Primrose Hill at dawn. **e) place to relax?** Yoga Class. **If you were asked to describe London to someone who had never been before, what would you say?** Big - Cold - Wild sides - Dull sides - Slowly becomes biggest village in England. If you plan on visiting London, come during the summer, between April and August. In winter it's grey skys are only broken with inner joy. If you are not entirely at one with yourself do not attempt to visit London during the winter months as you will become depressed. **Why do you love this city so much?** I didn't really choose London, but now that I've made my life here there's plenty to find to love about it. There's mad diversity in all of the every expanding waves of subculture variants. **Describe London in the:** *If the seasons were still in sync.* **a) Spring:** Expectant. **b) Summer:** Sexy & sweaty. **c) Autumn:** Brown & miserable. **d) Winter:** Grey & moody & smokey. **Tell us your best experience in the city.** Summer solstice sunrise on top of Primrose Hill and all the psychedelic years inside my tardis. **Which girl would you most like to see in Maharishi?** Janet Fischgrund because she is the true head of worldwide style and international fashion great white brotherhood. **Which boy would you most like to see in Maharishi?** Me. My first mission is to always create what I want to wear in a perfect world.

LONDON / Hardy Blechman + Maharishi in a Studio. Hardy.jpg / xstreaming balance & businesses / NEIL DAVENPORT

Name: Billy Biznizz. Age: Over 5, but under 50. Occupation: Turntablist. Residence: Brixton. How long have you lived in London? All my life. Where's the best: a) area? South London (Brixton) b) place to eat? Zara's Kitchen (Camberwell Green) c) place to socialise? Satay Bar d) place to party? Fridge Bar e) place to relax? Brockwell Park. If you were asked to describe London to someone who had never been before, what would you say? A cosmopolitan place with many things to see and do. Why do you love this city so much? Because it's helped shape me into what I am today. Describe London in the: a) spring: A chilled time to get ready for fun. b) summer: Fun with much female sight seeing. c) autumn: Quite mellowed out. d) winter: Drab. Tell us your best experience in the city. The birth of my son. Tell us your most memorable DJ spot, when, where and what went on. 1984-85 Rock Box with Nutroment, Pogo, Swift, Cosmic Jam, Quick Kut J, Live 2 Break, London Allstars, Mode2 and the Chrome Angels. One of the baddest B Boy Jams in the history of hip hop, all the elments of hip hop culture.

Blag Team Sally Edwards, Sarah Edwards, Chris Thomson, Richard Bull. blag@blag.demon.co.uk **Production** Call The Shots Ltd. **Design & Art Direction** Yacht Associates. **Legal Representation** Alex Betts, The Betts Partnership. **Visual Contributions** Mark Thomson, Untitled, Barnaby Wallace, Giant, Anat Stiendler, Kai Wiechmann, Andy Huckle, Ludvigsen, Inflate, Jason Tozer, Phil Knott, Tee Max, Jo Simpson, Red James, Trevor Roger, Sarah Edwards, Martyn Rose, David Jones, Neil Davenport, Sally Edwards, all other contributions by Yacht Associates. **Interviews and Q & A's** Sally Edwards, Ahmir Thompson, Mode 2. **Speller** Erik Slaholm. *Sally and Sarah would like to express their gratitude and love to the following people:* ABi...Afu-Ra...Alex Betts...Arsonists - Freestyle...Billy Biznizz...Black Eyed Peas: Will.I.Am, Taboo, Apl De Ap, Eddy & Yon...Bobbito...Die Gestalten Verlag...EPMD: Erick Sermon, Parish Smith & Bernard...Gary Aspden...Hardy Maharishi...Jungle Brothers: Mike G & Afrika Baby Bam...The Lost Boyz: Freaky Tah (RIP), Mr.Cheeks, Pretty Lou & Spigg Nice...Malik Izaak Taylor...Mike Giant...Mode 2...The Pharcyde: Romye, Imani, Greg, M-Walk & Tre...Phil Knott...Prince Paul...Redman & Chris Tricarico...The Roots: "The damn cute" Ahmir aka ?uestlove, Ranzel, Scratch, Tariq, Hub, Kamal, Malik B & Rich...Stum Village - Jay Dee, T3, Baatin & Timothy...Tee Max... Mucho respecto! Ajile...Becky Ford...Ben & Claire... Boudican...Carla Perillo...Cey Adams...Charlie Caplowe...Chuck D...Claude G...Duffy Family...Eddie Brannan... Eliott Waters...Fat Beats, Amsterdam...FLC: Skills, Fast & Huey...Fusion...Genius/GZA...Grand Royal: Dave, Katesy, Michael Diamond, Adam Yauch, Adam Horovitz & Kenny, The Tick...DJ Honda Crew...Independent Pictures' Cary Woods & Sofia Sondervan...Jefferson Hack...Jess Fleet...Kim Bull...Metropolis...Mix Master Mike...Mista Sinista...Natalie Carlson...Nihal & Simon...Normski & family...Patricia Niven...Professor Griff...Rankin...Rodney Hilton Smith...Rob & Matt...Ruth Robinson...Sam Hinks...Sarina...Scratch Perverts...Shane O'Neill... Shelby...Steph aka Princess...Tank...Treach...279...You...Loads of love to our lovely mum - Gillian Edwards & our big sis - Louise "Lou Lou" Edwards. *This wouldn't be possible without you ! This book is dedicated to Dad - William A H Edwards (RIP)* ©1999 Call The Shots Ltd. All rights reserved. No part of this publication may be reproduced in whole or part without permission from the publishers: Die Gestalten Verlag. The views expressed in blag are those of the respective contributors & are not necessarily shared by blag or its staff. Unless credited all photography & images © 1999 Yacht Associates.

CHEERS!

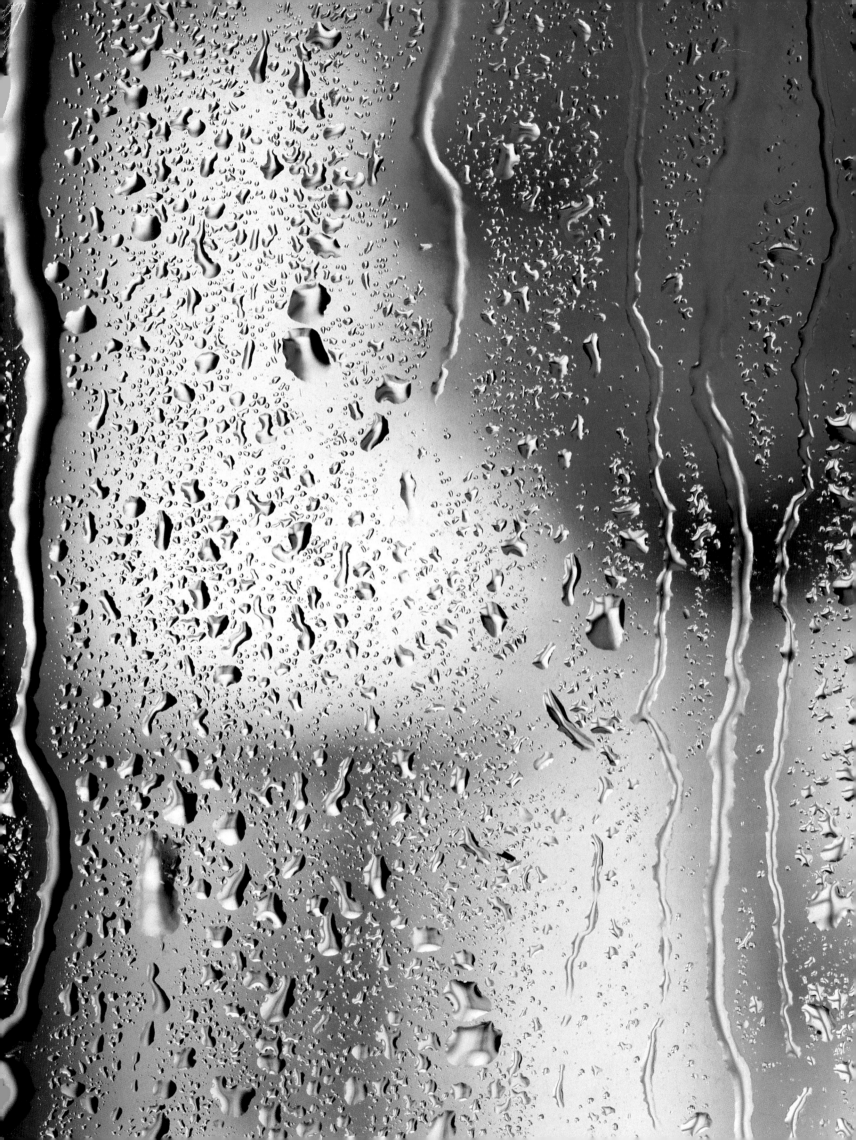

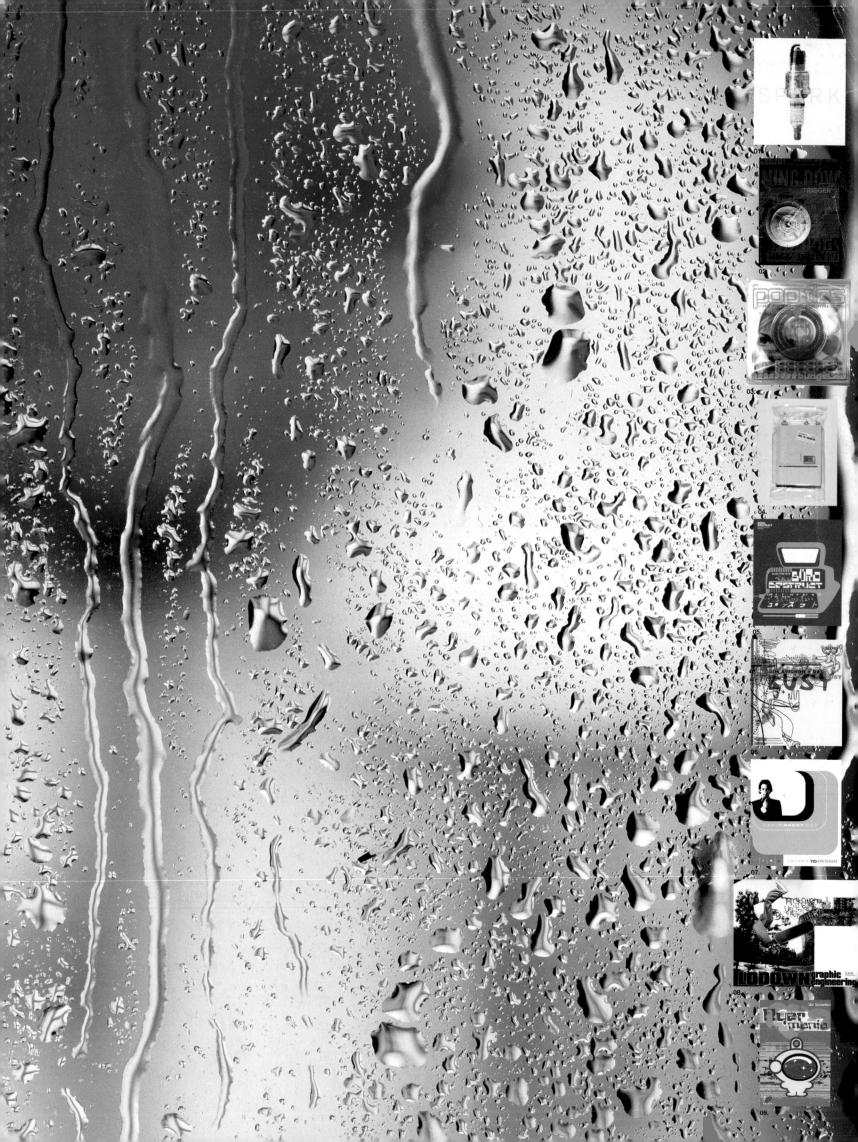